ZWINGLI, A REFORMED THEOLOGIAN

Zwingli

A REFORMED
THEOLOGIAN

Jaques
Courvoisier

THE ANNIE KINKEAD WARFIELD LECTURES OF 1961
PRINCETON THEOLOGICAL SEMINARY

JOHN KNOX PRESS
Richmond, Virginia

Library of Congress Catalog Card Number: 63-8064

1. Zwingli, Ulrich, 1484-1531

© M. E. Bratcher 1963
Printed in the United States of America
8773

To
the Universities of
Aberdeen and Saint Andrews
as a token of gratitude
for the degree of doctor of divinity
conferred upon the author.

Preface

The Annie Kinkead Warfield Lectures were established by Professor Benjamin B. Warfield in honor of his wife, in order that a series of lectures might be delivered each year at Princeton Theological Seminary on "some doctrine or doctrines of the Reformed system of doctrine." It was stipulated that the lectures should deal with "the biblical basis, or the historical development, or the systematic formulation, or the exposition or defense of said doctrine or doctrines."

In opening this series to a theologian who intended to treat some of the main features of the theology of Huldrych Zwingli, the Faculty of Princeton Seminary, which has responsibility for administering the Warfield Lectures, inferred that this subject was entirely within the intentions of the founder, and that such lectures could contribute to better understanding of a Reformer who is not yet known as he deserves to be.

Zwinglian studies have, in fact, developed in a remarkable way in the last forty years with the work of such scholars as Walther Koehler, Alfred and Oskar Farner (especially the latter), Fritz Blanke, Arthur Rich, Gottfried Locher, Rudolf Pfister, Julius Schweizer, Roger Ley, Heinrich Schmid, and others. But the thorough and illuminating researches of these men have not gained the circulation in the theological world they ought to have.

We hope to show in this book that Zwingli was what is properly called a Reformed theologian. A forerunner of Calvin in several realms of thought, he was a man with brilliant intuitions. In some cases, Zwingli went beyond the theological achievements of the Reformer of Geneva. Zwingli's broad intellectual horizons, and, in particular, what we have called the "ecclesial dimension" of his thought, have never been considered with the attention they ought to have drawn.

The five lectures represented in this volume are only outlines. Each opens up a topic worthy of much more profound and detailed study. Our hope is that some readers will find here an invitation and a stimulus to go further and to join the ranks of the Zwingli scholars.

We would like to express our gratitude to those who gave us the opportunity of presenting these lectures in the university town of Princeton: former President John A. Mackay, President James I. McCord, and Professor George S. Hendry, whose kindness, understanding, hospitality, and friendship remain for us a very happy remembrance. My deep gratitude goes to Walter J. Hollenweger, whose patience was put to the test in verifying my quotations, and, last but not least, to Lewis S. Mudge, who undertook the hard task of looking carefully at this text to make it readable in English.

J.C.

Geneva, April 1962

Contents

INTRODUCTION

Zwingli and the Swiss Reformation

Huldrych Zwingli was born in Wildhaus, Toggenburg, in the eastern part of Switzerland, on January 1, 1484. The village, where visitors may still see Zwingli's family house, transformed into a museum, is set on the mountain's flank, about 3600 feet above sea level. This house is a typical Swiss chalet: low, thick set, strongly held to the ground by heavy stones set on the roof to secure the dwelling in case of avalanche. Down in the valley runs the Thur, a tributary of the Rhine. From there, the panorama is wonderful: to the north the Säntis and to the south the Churfirsten. Life is hard but wholesome; winters last long. The ground is not good for cultivation, but only for pasture. The chief occupations are cattle raising and cultivating the forests for the sale of wood. The air is pure and healthy and the people are strong.

These folk love their country and the liberty they have, knowing how much it cost to be free from the landlords. At home, during the long winter evenings, gathered around the fireplace, the children listen to their parents' tales of preceding generations to whom they owe what they are. The young are enthusiastic when they hear of the heroic deeds of their ancestors who fought to be free. It is here that our future Reformer began to love his country so intensely.

Zwingli was a good specimen of this Alpine people: highly colored, dumpy, strong, with energetic chin and lively glance. He was proud to be a peasant and to be totally such. According to him, those who work the ground resemble the Creator more than other men. "Keep the nobility you inherited from Adam"[1] (regarded as the first peasant), he wrote once to his brothers, "as it is among peasants that you will find more peace and virtue than elsewhere."[2]

During his childhood, and each time he found himself again in his mountains, he observed nature keenly, and reflectively directed his thoughts toward its author. Later on, in his preaching, one can easily find the echo of what he noticed: "Does not the tribe of mice proclaim God's wisdom and providence? And the hedgehog which rolls himself up like a ball and ingeniously gathers his provision of fruit into his den on his quills?" "Do not mountains—this tragic, overwhelming and mysterious mass—proclaim God's mighty power and majesty, as holding the earth together, as the bones do the flesh?"[3]

Zwingli's way of speaking was influenced by his surroundings. It is rather difficult to translate it into another language. In his mouth, the "green pastures" (Ps. 23) become beautiful Alpine meadows (In schöner Alp weidet er mich). "The streams in the south" (Ps. 126:4, K.J.V.) become the frozen brooks over which the southern wind (foehn) blows. In temptation, the believer has to be like the snail re-entering its shell.[4]

Zwingli was a man of good sense. "It is not possible to confide in God and in the Saints at the same time. Otherwise, one is like those children who are asked, 'Whom do you prefer in the family?' and they answer, 'Father.' But if the mother adds: 'I thought it was I,' the children answer: 'We prefer you too!' In the end they would say the same thing to the maid."[5]

This shrewd peasant was a fine musician. We are told that he used to play seven different musical instruments. His skill was so great that when the children he had to teach were noisy, he used to play to keep them quiet; and he succeeded!

The Reformer's father and grandfather had been mayors of Wildhaus and the priesthood was highly valued in this notable family. Two uncles of Zwingli's were priests, and among the eleven children of this large household, five (three boys and two girls) were chosen to enter orders. Huldrych was soon sent to live with his uncle Bartholomaeus, dean in Weesen, on the shore of Lake Walenstadt. He went to school there and was such a good pupil that soon afterward his uncle sent him to Basle, and thence after two years to Berne where he spent the same length of time. It was in Berne that he studied with Wölflin (Lupulus), a distinguished humanist, who introduced him to the study of classical antiquity.

Urged to enter the Dominican monastery of this town, where music was highly cultivated, Zwingli, on his family's entreaties, gave up the idea as a temptation. He continued his studies in Vienna, then came back to Basle where he remained from 1502 to 1506, to complete his course. He took the degrees of bachelor and master of arts, respectively, in 1504 and 1506. During the same years, he became acquainted with the famous printer Froben. To a certain extent, this environment was not too favorable for a future cleric. In that epoch, one was either humanist or theologian, either cultivated or priest! But in his last year of study Zwingli fortunately came in contact with Thomas Wyttenbach, of Biel. Wyttenbach was perhaps the man who had the greatest influence upon him. Thanks to him, according to Zwingli himself, he got rid "of the sophist's vain babbling" and found the link between study and the pastoral ministry.

On September 29, 1506, Zwingli, as an ordained priest, celebrated his first Mass in his native village. At the year's end, he was settled as a curate in Glarus. He was twenty-two years old and approached his ministerial work in a very conventional way, according to the rules of the church. In the course of the summer of 1516, for instance, he could have been seen at the head of a procession, bearing the sacred host, in order to ask God for fine weather after a rainy season.

Zwingli was a faithful curate. "Though I was young," he wrote in 1523, "ecclesiastical duties inspired in me more fear than joy, because I knew, and I remained convinced, that I would have to give account of the blood of the sheep which would perish as a consequence of my carelessness."[6]

The young curate combined academic study with pastoral care. In the parish house, the ground floor was the dwelling of the priest, where he acted as such, meeting his parishioners, fasting and praying, while on the second floor was his study, where he

carried on the practice of Latin and Greek, becoming more and
more familiar with the classical documents of antiquity.

From the moral point of view, this strongly constituted man
had difficulties with sex. He failed in this respect. But he knew
how to get himself under control again and, according to his own
statement, remained in chastity six months or even one year at a
time, notwithstanding the fact that "temptations were not missing." While in Zurich he was married, and it is recorded that he
was a good husband and a good father.

Patriotism was a noticeable feature of Zwingli's life. It is not
astonishing that this sentiment was so strongly expressed in his
ministry. Patriotic feeling led him to fight against the mercenary
service of Swiss soldiers in foreign countries from the very beginning of his career. Zwingli disliked war. As a military chaplain in
the Italian war, he had been at Monza and Marignan. He shared
for a while the political ideas of Cardinal Schiner, a remarkable
diplomat and a faithful servant of the pope. But in the end, Zwingli went his own way and became a strong opponent of every
alliance with foreign powers, including that of the pope, giving
back the papal pension he had been granted some years previously. At that time, the Swiss were well-known for their military
qualifications and highly prized as mercenaries by European
princes. And since Switzerland was poor from the agricultural
point of view, foreign service was a source of income for the
country. Swiss soldiers, lured by the possibility of adventure,
plunder, and glory, enlisted. They brought back, if not riches, at
least many "souvenirs" for which they were admired, especially
by the female part of the population. Money became more plen-
tiful, but at the same time bad habits and rough language in-
creased. In the end, the whole country was in danger of demoral-
ization in the proper sense of the word; for men who remained
in the country as peasants were regarded, even by themselves, as
stupid people, earning by hard labor a living which could be
gained more easily in foreign wars.

Fighting against this mercenary service, Zwingli was defend-
ing the spiritual welfare of his country. The foreign princes, with
their gold, were in his view nothing else than birdlime. "The

situation is very serious; we are already contaminated. Religion is in danger of ceasing to exist among us. We despise God as if he were an old sleepy dog. . . Yet, it was only by his power that our fathers overcame their enemies because they went to war for their liberties, and not for money. . . Now, puffed with pride, we pretend that nobody can resist us, as if we were strong as iron and our foes slack as pumpkins." Such a struggle against mercenary service had, indeed, its moral aspect: "If a foreign soldier violently bursts in, ravages your fields and vineyards, carries off your cattle, puts your magistrates under arrest, kills your sons who stand up to defend you, violates your daughters, kicks your wife to get rid of her, murders your old servant hiding himself in the granary, has no consideration for your supplications, and finally sets your house on fire, you think that earth ought to open and swallow him up and you ask yourself if God really exists . . . But if you are doing the same thing to other people, you say: Such is war! What is a warrior? Euripides said, 'At war, he who thinks a man is more than a frog is nothing. . .' " [7] Therefore, a break must be made with these foreign princes. "Whether they are our allies or our enemies we will eventually get the worst of it and in the end be dishonored. Keep away, Switzerland, from foreign powers, for they are leading you to ruin!" [8]

Such a clear judgment upon war did not prevent Zwingli from being a soldier to his boots. Strongly against wars of conquest, he nonetheless knew that Swiss liberties had been achieved by force of arms. If he loved peace, he did not love just any peace, and certainly not the kind of peace which left old people, women, and children without protection. It was indispensable in his view to be adequately armed to keep them safe and, with them as well as for them, the native soil. Defensive war could be carried on with good conscience. With such opinions, Zwingli was one of the originators of the Swiss policy of armed neutrality which has played an important role in safeguarding the independence of the nation throughout subsequent history.

Zwingli and Luther were almost the same age. Zwingli was one year younger. The reformations they were to carry out happened

at nearly the same time. It is well known, furthermore, that both
reforming movements followed immediately upon the burst of
humanism of which Erasmus had been the most brilliant representative.

Having received his academic training from the humanists,
Zwingli held to their methods throughout his life, particularly
their habit of going back to sources and their rigorous intellectual discipline. But having walked harmoniously for a time, humanists and Reformers drew apart and finally became enemies.
There are, indeed, fundamental differences between these currents
of thought. Where humanism saw in Jesus Christ the master,
the paragon of virtue, the Reformation saw in him the Saviour
who forgives and vouchsafes everlasting life. Where humanism
regarded the Gospel as a code for sinless life, the Reformation
saw a given righteousness, a righteousness imputed by God to
man. Humanism knows morality, says Walther Koehler, in substance, but it misses the power behind it.[9]

Zwingli and Erasmus were for a while rather close friends. But
after a serious row concerning Ulrich von Hutten, one of the
German knights who for a time took the humanist side only to
be unceremoniously dropped by Erasmus, the two took their dis-
tance from each other and at last broke. Subsequently, at the
Dispute of Baden in 1526, Erasmus helped the famous Dr. Eck of
Ingolstadt, likewise an opponent of Luther, to oppose Zwingli,
using arguments which aggravated the subsequent disagreement
at Marburg between the German and Swiss Reformers. When a
decision was to be taken the great humanist was openly on the
Roman Catholic side.

At any rate, the day came when the humanist Zwingli discovered that the Christian religion is to be understood not simply as
the most perfect of the faiths of men, but as the link between
him who says to Moses, "I am who I am," and humanity. Religion
ceased to be mere concept and became God's call to mankind.
"Adam, where art thou?" From that time, religion for Zwingli
was nothing but this divine initiative. At that moment, if such
a comparison is relevant, Zwingli, who had been sitting among
the humanists watching an interesting theatrical performance,

left his seat and jumped onto the stage to take his part in what was going on. Now he had to "live" the Reformation.

One may be puzzled by the fact that, at this moment, Zwingli did not join Luther, who fundamentally had the same attitude. But Zwingli and Luther were very different. There was between them the chasm which separates the Swiss from the German (greater than the non-Swiss can imagine). The Swiss were democrats and, as such, were despised by the Germans, who felt themselves superior because they had princes ruling over them. From the philosophical point of view, Luther was educated in the nominalist, Scotist position while Zwingli was more or less a realist; Luther was not a humanist, whereas Zwingli fundamentally was. Certainly Zwingli admired Luther. He called him the "Elijah" of the Reformation, or the "David who killed the Roman wild bear," or even a soldier of God "who scrutinizes the Scriptures with such accuracy that a man like him is hardly to be found every thousand years."[10] Zwingli, for example, wholly agreed with the Lutheran doctrine of justification by faith, as Calvin did a generation later.

Nevertheless, Zwingli clearly pointed out that he was not to be considered a Lutheran. If he said what Luther said, it was because "they both drank at the same source." "Why don't you call me a Paulinian since I am preaching like Saint Paul. . . . I do not want to be labeled a Lutheran by the Papists, as it is not Luther who taught me the doctrine of Christ, but the Word of God. If Luther preaches Christ, he does the same thing as I do. Therefore, I will not bear any name save that of my chief, Jesus Christ, whose soldier I am."[11]

But the greater and more fundamental difference between the two Reformers lay perhaps in the starting points of their thinking. Where Luther says, "How shall *I* be saved?", Zwingli says, "How will *my people,* my nation, be saved?" The main preoccupation of Luther, either in Erfurt or in Wittenberg, was his soul's salvation. There was nothing egoistic in this, of course, as Luther was bearing, so to speak, the whole anxiety of his epoch. But Zwingli's concern was principally salvation for the Swiss nation. Arthur Rich, in a very suggestive book,[12] recalls that Zwingli, on

the occasion of an epidemic of plague in which he came close to
death, reflected on the coincidence between his own mortal illness
and the sickness of his people which could lead to spiritual death.
Zwingli's recovery was conversely compared with the success of
the Reformation—*Christianismus renascens*—in the church.

Intense communication with the biblical authors made Zwingli
the Reformer history knows. Oswald Myconius, his close friend,
fellow laborer, and earliest biographer, wrote this statement: "... in the judgment of learned persons, he was a thorough
master of the Holy Scriptures, but, unlike the scholars of his day,
he needed more and more the knowledge of original languages,
for he knew that only such knowledge could fill certain gaps.
To begin with, he devoted himself to the study of Greek litera-
ture... For his personal use, he copied out all the Pauline letters,
to soak himself in them. He reached the point of understanding
Paul better in Greek than in Latin. Later, he did the same with
all the other books of the New Testament. He learned from
Peter (2 Peter 1:21) that interpretation of Scripture is beyond
the unaided capacities of the children of men and he looked above
to his master, the Holy Spirit, praying that he make him understand God's thoughts aright. And in order not to err, or lead
others astray with a false picture of the Spirit, he compared scriptural passages with each other, explaining the obscure ones with
the clear ones. In order that everybody could recognize the Holy
Spirit's teaching, as opposed to that of human wisdom... Thus,
knowledge of the Scriptures, so long suppressed to the detri-
ment of men's souls, was reinstated in the happiest possible
way."[13]

Zwingli the Reformer is not to be considered apart from
Zwingli the pastor. In the midst of a dangerous life, punctuated
by attempts to kidnap or kill him, he always thought and acted
as a soldier. He had a preference for military language, which is
typical of the Swiss, and described the pastor with his weapon,
the Word of God, and his armor as having nothing to fear (*Nicht
fürchten ist der Harnisch*). The pastor, as he wrote in a book
called *The Shepherd (Der Hirt)*, is a warrior who ought to de-
vote himself to God's service. The ministry is a battle under

Christ's command. He is the paragon of the pastor in his life as
well as in his death. Under his leadership, the pastor will attack
every fortress erected against the Word of God. He will speak to
the great men of this world as Elijah, Jeremiah, or John the
Baptist used to do. He will engage himself totally, even for the
weakest of his sheep. He will remember that the cross is at the
end of his road, as he speaks generally to people "who have in
their own opinions the same pleasure the she monkey finds in
her little ones." All this will be accomplished in the love the
pastor has for those who have been entrusted to him. If "he gives
salt to some of his sheep and kicks others," he will still love them
all, reflecting God's love. Everything must be orientated by this
love and be measured by it. Courage, skill, and even faith are
nothing without love. Is such a way difficult? Perhaps, for it leads
to self-sacrifice and death. But if so, God has truly protected the
pastor "because nobody suffers death for God who does not be-
long to him. Here you will learn the foundation of faith and
love. Do you believe there is one God almighty and one alone?
Do you believe also that he is your God, your Lord, and your
Father? Do you trust him entirely? If so, you will truly believe,
without any doubt, that what he promised you will be vouchsafed. . . If you look upon him as a father, you will love him
and, if so, you will not tolerate that his honor be attacked, his
word not trusted, or that people live against his will. Would you
suffer death rather than endure your father's shame? The more
so, for your heavenly Father! If you believe that the Word of
God cannot lie, you will at the same time know that on earth,
the greatest honor granted by the heavenly Father to one of his
sons is to allow him to die in his service."[14]

At the beginning of 1519, Zwingli was appointed curate at the
Zurich cathedral, the Grossmünster. A small, clean town of seven
thousand inhabitants on the Limmat river and at the end of the
lake of the same name, Zurich had achieved its liberties by conquest and was governed by town authorities which, imperceptibly,
had become state authorities. The bishop dwelt in Constance, a
town belonging to the Holy Roman Empire, and he therefore

had little interest in this part of his diocese, which was, in effect, in another country. Certain tensions soon developed between Zwingli and the bishop concerning questions which were minor indeed to begin with but eventually led to rupture. Such a break with the bishop did not mean excommunication, but simply that Zwingli was no longer entitled to be curate of the Grossmünster. The council of Zurich was not at all happy with this development, as the city had become more and more attached to such an intelligent, patriotic, and skillful preacher. The council, therefore, took the unprecedented and rather bold step of appointing Zwingli, on its own authority, as a preacher in the same cathedral, without suspecting that it was thus inaugurating the first evangelical ministry. But the Reformation was not officially established at that moment, and even if perceptive people realized that fundamental changes were on the way nobody could anticipate the true extent of what was to happen.

A dispute, held in January 1523, was the occasion for further steps forward. Such meetings were usual in this period. Generally, they were convened by the magistrate in order that opposing viewpoints could confront each other publicly and a decision be made on the basis of the issues. In fact, the decision of the authorities was already taken before the dispute. Such gatherings were only organized when the government had made up its mind to go forward. They nevertheless had the advantage of explaining to the public what was to be done and of launching the new action. Dignitaries of the church were invited to this particular dispute, notably the bishop who sent his representative, the general vicar Faber. Zwingli was asked to prepare theses as a basis for discussion. The expected result ensued, and was proclaimed. Some months later a second dispute, less important than the first, sharpened the previous results on the basis of experience acquired in the meantime.

In carrying on partial reforms, the Zurich authorities acted carefully and even tactfully, certainly more so than was subsequently the case in several places. Paintings and statues were removed from the churches while stained glass was allowed to remain, as it could not be an object of worship. Monks and nuns were given the opportunity to leave their monasteries, but those who wanted to remain were allowed to do so. For the latter, two monasteries were set apart, one for women and the other for men. Meanwhile, in 1524, the abbess of the Frau-münster, Catherine von Zimmern, solemnly gave her abbey with all the perquisites attached to it, including her sovereign rights possessed since the time of Charlemagne's grandson, Louis the German, to the town authorities. From then on, changes occurred gradually, so gradually indeed that Mass was only abolished in Zurich in 1525, two years after the dispute, and professed Romanists were still allowed to be members of the city council until 1529.

The soul of this Reformation was the so-called "Prophecy," an idea of Zwingli's which was later to be imitated as far away as England, with some differences. Each morning, at seven o'clock, the preachers, former canons, chaplains, and elder students of the Latin schools gathered in the choir of the cathedral to study the Old Testament. A young participant read the text of the day in Latin from the Vulgate. Then a teacher read it in Hebrew and explained it. A third read it again from the Septuagint, in Greek. A fourth then discussed the text in Latin and indicated how it ought to be preached in church. The doors were then opened to the public and a fifth participant preached on the text in Swiss German.[15]

It is easy to see, from such an example, how far reformation was based on the assumption that Holy Scripture should be put in the hands of the people and clearly explained. It was in the midst of this "Prophecy," nucleus of the Zurich academy, pattern and starting point for all the Reformed academies, that a work of translation and exegesis was carried out which resulted, in 1529, in the publication of the Zurich Bible, one of the most important contributions to posterity by the ministers of that town.

The Zurich Reformation was carried out on two fronts, the Roman one, of course, and the Anabaptist. The latter aspect of the struggle ought not to be minimized because it was more quickly resolved. In the Anabaptists, Zwingli met adversaries who thought that he was not going fast enough or far enough in his work. According to them, radical changes in the church were needed. Their premises were different from those of the Reformers. According to the Anabaptists the historic and established church had to be replaced by an entirely new one constituted solely of individually converted members—already the formula of the Pietist movement. According to Anabaptist ideas, baptism as administered in the Roman Church was void. The Roman communion was not entitled to be considered as a church, and, furthermore, one could only be baptized as a conscious believer, confessing the Lord's name. True believers had to retire from human society. A Christian could not be a magistrate. They were forbidden to take oaths before the civil courts, because of Christ's commandment to say "yes" or "no" and nothing more.

Zwingli was very far from sharing such views. For him, the church had not to be destroyed but reformed in order to be the herald of the Gospel, in the midst of a society always regarded as Christian. Without the church, this society could not stand. Zwingli developed his ideas in a treatise, *On Divine and Human Justice*. Zwingli's activity met great difficulties at the hands of the Anabaptists, difficulties which were largely overcome with the help of the government by 1526, after the application of very stern measures. Some Anabaptists were banished and others drowned in the river.

Zwingli's work was given still more precision, both in his struggle against Anabaptists and Roman Catholics, and in the maintenance of the church, by the creation of an ecclesiastical discipline and especially of a matrimonial tribunal. The year after, in 1526, the latter became a court of morals, the true ancestor of the Genevan Consistory.[16] The establishment of a real civil registry dates from this epoch.

Reformation in Zurich was bound to have its echo outside, in the rest of Switzerland. The Swiss Confederation was, at that moment, composed of thirteen sovereign cantons bound to each other by regularly renewable covenants and by a diet which met alternatively in certain designated towns. The cantons collaborated in the administration of their common subject territories. These territories had been conquered by the confederates who, after the conquest of Aargau in 1415, decided to maintain their conquests jointly and to commit them to the administration of bailiffs appointed in turn by the different cantons.

These territories were apples of discord in Reformation times. Depending on the canton which had to appoint him, the bailiff might hold either the old faith or the new one. The confessional climate might thus change repeatedly in the same territory. Other misunderstandings came from the federal covenants themselves. They included no confessional stipulations, having been concluded before the Reformation. But everybody knew that the Swiss cantons were within Christendom: that is, they belonged to the institutional Roman Church, the only existing one. The most famous covenant, that of 1291, which marked, in effect, the origin of Switzerland, had been established "in the name of the Lord." Now, with the Reformation unfolding in Zurich, the cantons which remained faithful to the pope denied the city the right to be still considered a member of the Western Catholic Church. From its point of view, Zurich stated strongly that it belonged to the church more authentically than the other cantons, having rediscovered the Word of God. Troubles arose as a consequence which were quickly turned into acts of violence: iconoclasm, monasteries set on fire, Reformed pastors arrested when crossing Roman Catholic cantons, burnings at the stake, executions. Finally, Zurich was isolated and excluded from the renewal of the covenants.

The situation was further complicated by economic difficulties in the Roman Catholic cantons. Zurich and Berne (won to the Reformation in 1528) were richer than they. Tension was growing of a kind which could only lead to war. The first conflict burst out in 1529, but was ended without any open recourse to battle. Zwingli gained the advantage in this case, but remained deeply worried because his opponents kept their forces intact. In the following months, the Roman Catholic cantons appealed for aid out of exasperation at the economic blockade imposed on them by Zurich and Berne.

Outside Switzerland the situation of German Protestants was precarious. This was clear from what appeared at the Diet of Speyer in 1529. The same year, an attempt at Marburg to achieve theological agreement between Luther and Zwingli in order to present a united Protestant front had failed.

In this situation, Zwingli conceived the stratagem of building a European alliance of countries which naturally feared the growth of the Holy Roman Empire. Starting with the idea "Papacy and Empire are both from Rome,"[17] he pointed out that the dominance of one political power in Europe could not be but connected with the exclusive dominion of one confession: the Roman one. Consequently, to safeguard the liberty of the Gospel, he aimed at an alliance of powers which had an interest in resisting the Empire. With the Landgraf of Hesse, the German prince who had convened the colloquy at Marburg, he projected an alliance extending from Denmark to Venice, including Hesse, Strassburg, Wurtemberg, Switzerland, and France, to provide a wall along the axis of the Rhine behind which the liberty of preaching would be safe. The plan was not to succeed for many reasons, among them the fact that France refused to take it seriously.[18]

In the meantime, however, reformation had gained a firm foothold in Switzerland. Basle had been won and above all Berne, the canton which held the balance of power in the Confederation. But Berne was nonetheless reluctant, for it seemed to them that Zwingli was going too fast and too far. His eventual project, to make Berne and Zurich the governing powers of Switzerland "like two oxen under the same yoke," was not at all welcomed by the lords of this canton. In Zurich itself, the inhabitants were less and less inclined to bear the burden of ecclesiastical discipline. They became downhearted at the deteriorating appearance of events. Zwingli himself, aware of the situation, went so far as to offer his resignation. The offer was not accepted by the Council.

A second civil war was in the offing, for which the Roman Catholic cantons had carefully prepared in the hope of revenge. It burst out in 1531 and this time blood was shed. Berne had prudently kept its forces far from the probable battlefield. Zurich went forth alone to fight, unfortunately unprepared, and this time was beaten. Zwingli, who was among the troops as a chaplain, was killed.

Information concerning his death is to be found in the writings of Myconius, Bucer, and Bullinger. They state that Zwingli, seeing some of his people overwhelmed by a great number of enemies, threw himself actively into the battle to either save them or die with them. Hit several times, he fell and, in the evening after the battle, was found by the victorious soldiers, lying on the ground, dying, unable to speak, hands joined as for prayer, eyes raised to heaven. Identified as a "heretic" he was reviled and finally killed by a captain from Unterwald. His body was then burned and his ashes scattered.

"It makes no difference," he said as he fell, "they can kill the body but not the soul!"[19]

Was Zwingli's death to destroy the Reformer's work? History answers "no." A man can be killed, but not his ideas. Zwingli's spiritual heritage was gathered up by Bullinger, later by Bucer, and finally by Calvin, who owed more to him than he thought. Moreover, if Berne was cool to Zwingli's politics, it remained firmly attached to reformation. Berne, thanks to its political power, was to sponsor the expansion of the new ideas to the territories which today constitute the French-speaking part of Switzerland. Because of this, the Reformation was established and maintained in Geneva and from there it reached France. If it had not been for Berne, Calvin's work in Geneva would have been unthinkable. And from Calvin, English and Scottish refugees, to mention only these nationalities, were able to learn what they were later to bring to their own countries. If Presbyterianism and Puritanism derived anything from Calvin's Geneva, and if they were important in history, Berne and ultimately Zwingli played a vital role in making it possible. For here was the movement which, according to the Swiss historian Ernst Gagliardi, was "by far the mightiest influence stemming from Switzerland upon the entire outside world."[20]

I

THE WORD OF GOD

The Reference to the Word of God

In his commentary *On True and False Religion (De vera et falsa religione)*, Zwingli insists that the "true source" of all religion, "e.g., faith, life, God's commandments, worship, and the sacraments," is the Word of God. The Reformation as a whole was based on this principle, at least in the Reformers' intentions, and any study of Zwingli's theology ought therefore to begin with his understanding of the Word.[1]

The Bible gives a special place to the Word of God in the midst of his whole work. When God creates the world, he speaks. He does nothing else. "At the beginning of creation, God said, 'Let there be light,' and there was light (Gen. 1:3). Notice that the light, called in this manner, did not just appear arbitrarily, but came into existence out of nothingness, in order to obey the Word of its Creator."[2] Such a Word implies an interlocutor. Zwingli saw in the Word of God, in the act of creation, a sign that God speaks to himself in the economy of the Trinity. Besides, he underlined the fact that, creating man in his own image, God created him fit to hear the Word he speaks. But Zwingli did not interpret our creation in God's image to mean that man, considering what he is and what he knows of himself, can grasp God's being directly. Man has never and will never see God in an external way. The *imago dei*, essentially, has to do with man's soul—not with its essence or substance but with its attributes such as will, understanding, and memory, considered as signs of the *imago* and reflecting it as in a mirror (1 Cor.

13:12).[3] Indeed, "We know as little about God as a beetle knows about man. Moreover, God is incomparably further from man than man is from the beetle. . . When they deal with the essence of God, the philosophical borrowings of the theologians are a swindle. They are false religion." If pagans have spoken the truth about God, it is because God has dropped some seeds of knowledge of himself among them. "As for us, because God has spoken to us by his Son and by the Holy Spirit, we do not need to look for knowledge of him among the wise men of this world. . . We need only look in his Word."[4]

If it is impossible for man, on his own, to achieve knowledge of God, it is just as difficult for him to know himself—as difficult as to "catch an octopus" (which emits a kind of ink in self-defense). Man's sole knowledge of man is to be found in the revelation God gives him in Jesus Christ. "Man only knows the secrets of the human heart under God's direction."[5] Man must look close to God for knowledge of himself as well as of his Creator.[6]

The analogy here could well be called an analogy of *relation*. God reveals himself to man so that man understands. Man finds in himself, on the basis of what revelation teaches him, a kind of reflection, or imperfect image, of what God really is. Thus memory, understanding, and will become signs of God's nature. And the Word implying divine-human contact makes the analogy between God and ourselves concrete.

The Word of God sets us apart from the other living beings: animals and plants. Man has in common with God not only the fact that he is gifted with memory, intelligence, and will, but also the fact that he directs "his attention toward God and his Word,"[7] doing so by his human nature and qualifications.[8]

Here, the word "nature" raises an inescapable question: Does Zwingli argue in terms of an analogy of the being *(analogia entis)*? Does he embrace natural theology? The Reformer clarifies his thought immediately: The "nature" in virtue of which we aspire after God is not that "of the flesh or of temptation but that which goes with God's image stamped in us by the divine artisan."[9] For Zwingli, "nature" is what God originally created, i.e., man's status as he was first fashioned, having received the

breath of life, "which is not weak" like man's breath.[10] This
status was soon afterward corrupted by the fall.

Since the fall, the Word, which is at the same time the power
of God, is especially adapted to man's needs. Revelation brings us
exactly what God wanted from us when he first created us. Thus,
the regenerated man, fit to hear and to acknowledge God's Word
as such, "finds his pleasure in the law of God because he has
been created in God's own image," and, to the extent that this
is so, "the inward man rejoices in no other law or word than
that of God."[11] This is why Christ, recalling Deuteronomy 8:3,
says: "Man shall not live by bread alone, but by every word that
proceedeth out of the mouth of God."[12] Zwingli, like other
Reformers such as Bucer, and later Calvin, uses a comparison
drawn from John 10:4: Man recognizes the voice of God the way
a sheep recognizes the call of its shepherd.

There is, then, something in us which corresponds to God,
something which comes from the fact that we were originally
created in God's own image, and which refuses to be bound to
our carnal nature since the latter has been wounded and in-
delibly marked by sin.[13]

There is no point of contact here pre-established between
God and us *(Anknupfungspunkt)*. Zwingli is talking about the
recognition of God's Word in the measure to which man, originally created in God's image, becomes conscious of this Word
by faith; in other terms, in the extent to which we are regenerated by God's gracious initiative. We rejoice in the Word of
God, for this is, *par excellence,* the way God reveals himself to
us and awakens us to awareness of it. The Word of God thus belongs to God alone, and is exclusively a matter of his own creative
or redemptive initiative.

How Does the Word of God Come to Us?

Through Jesus Christ

In the introductory pages of his treatise *On the Clarity and
Certitude of the Word of God (Von Klarheit und gewüsse oder
unbetrogliche des Worts Gottes,* 1522), formerly a sermon preached

before the Dominican nuns of Oetenbach (Zurich), Zwingli writes as follows: "This sermon is intended to show the foundations on which the whole edifice is to be erected, namely the Word of God . . . as Paul says: 'For no other foundation can anyone lay than that which is laid, which is Jesus Christ'" (1 Cor. 3:11).[14] Later Zwingli adds, alluding to John 1:9, "that the Word, or Son of God, was the true light which lighteth every man."[15] Zwingli then twice affirms an identity between Jesus Christ and the Word of God himself, just as only this light has the power to illuminate men. He who pretends to supply his own light here is turned away. The story of the Samaritan woman (John 4:25) is evidence that men with their wisdom do not understand anything about Christ while this woman, believing Jesus' own words, confesses that he is the Christ.[16]

If we have wondered how far Zwingli based his thought on natural theology, we see from these passages that he did not do so at all, that he rejected it energetically when fundamental questions were involved.

Through the Gospel

The Gospel is something which has not entered into the heart of man (cf. 1 Cor. 2:9), whose aim is to open man's understanding for the comprehension of Scripture. Zwingli defines it as follows: ". . . not only what Matthew, Mark, Luke, and John have written, but all that God has ever revealed to men."[17] In the *Exposition of the Sixty-Seven Theses (Auslegung der Schlussreden, 1523)*, Art. 16, he says that everything God reveals to man and demands of him is Gospel—Gospel rather than Law,[18] for the promise always goes with the Law[19] and because these things become clearer from the standpoint of the believer, Christ being sum and substance of salvation and thus salvation itself. The Gospel includes Law, promise, and fulfillment "because all these things are eternal and are wrapped up in the good news of salvation."[20]

As soon as there is an encounter between God and man through the Word of God, there is Gospel, good news, because "the sum of the Gospel is that our Lord Jesus Christ, the true

Son of God, has revealed to us the will of his heavenly Father, saving us from death by his innocence and reconciling us with God."[21] God's revelation converges upon this good news; more, it is essentially the good news itself.

The Gospel is a way of speaking of the dealings of God through Christ with us from the very creation of the world. Just as God created man through his Son (one may notice here again the identity between the Son and the Word), he also decided to redeem fallen man through his Son. Creation and redemption ought always to be held together (John 1:3; Col. 1:16-20).[22]

With Paul, Zwingli describes the Gospel as the power of God (Rom. 1:16). Similarly, in creation, the Word is God's act. For God, word and act are not separated as they are in man. In redemption, the proclaimed Gospel actually effects the believer's salvation, for with God, proclamation and effective action are the same thing.[23]

The Gospel, therefore, really is good news—that is, something not known before which one learns at the very moment one experiences its benefits. The very essence of the Gospel is that sins are forgiven in the name of Jesus Christ, and only in him. If man could reach God any other way, Jesus' death would have been completely useless.[24]

The Gospel, then, is something which man cannot discover on his own. Its purpose, as Christ's teaching of his disciples at Emmaus shows (Luke 24), is to open our minds to the true understanding of Holy Scripture.[25]

We thus reach the third dimension of Zwingli's concept of the Word of God.

Through Holy Scripture

Zwingli, like the other Reformers, argued on the basis of the Bible. Why? Because "those who do not know the Scriptures ought to be taken by the nose and, as Christ commands, compelled to scrutinize them," in order "to feel clearly the easiness of his yoke and the lightness of his burden."[26]

Giving such advice, Zwingli follows the example of Christ, who sends us back to the Scriptures because they bear witness to him (John 5:39-41).[27] This preference for the Bible is exclusive, for only the Holy Spirit, not men, can teach us all things and remind us what Christ said. Indeed, "though the Word is proclaimed by men, it is not a human word; it will not reach human hearts if God does not draw them to him."[28] But we know from God's promises that he will indeed speak to the hearts of men. This divine assurance is the *raison d'être* of preaching.

All that we know about the Word of God comes from the Scriptures. What is said there concerning God is clear.[29] In spite of every possible distinction between human language and divine there is a close link—so close, so to speak, that nothing can separate the two—between the Word of God and Holy Scripture. Thanks to God's promise, indeed, there is no exaggeration in virtually identifying them. "When I am looking for a real touchstone," says Zwingli, "I do not find any other than the stone of stumbling and the rock of offence (cf. 1 Peter 2:8, K.J.V.) which trips up those who nullify God's commandments like the Pharisees. Consequently, from the start [Zwingli here recalls the beginning of his career], I have put every doctrine to the test at this stone. . ." And he concludes: "Holy Scripture must be our guide and teacher; he who uses Scripture rightly will be free from God's reproach."[30] Thus the touchstone is simultaneously Jesus Christ, the Gospel,[31] and Holy Scripture. Through his Word, God, the object of faith, implants this faith in the human heart.[32]

It is sometimes difficult to see any distinction between the Word of God and Holy Scripture in Zwingli's writing. The problem preoccupies him no more than it does the other Reformers. Like them, Zwingli sometimes goes from one term to the other in seeming confusion. But it is precisely in the dialectical movement from one to the other that his teaching is to be grasped in both cases, for the Word of God manifests itself *in* Scripture and *in relation to* it. Then, if a council does not err, it will be because "nothing is decided save what Scripture, filled with the Spirit of God, teaches."[33]

Grounded upon the Bible, Zwingli is thus grounded upon the

Word of God, that is to say, upon the good news of salvation in Jesus Christ. He will be led by the Holy Spirit as far as he will rely exclusively upon it.

The Power of the Word of God

"For God's sake," says Zwingli, "do not put yourself at odds with the Word of God. For truly, it will persist as surely as the Rhine follows its course. One can perhaps dam it up for a while, but it is impossble to stop it."[34] As an observer of nature, Zwingli finds the appropriate analogy. "The Word of God is so strong and certain that, when God commands, everything obeys at once. God's Word is so lively and so mighty that all things, including inanimate objects and irrational beings, conform themselves to it instantaneously. Better said, all things, rational or not, because they are shaped by him, are destined and directed as he himself has decided."[35] "An eternal power radiates from God's Word." The Old Testament and the New prove this, and show that "nature would collapse rather than let the Word of God not be accomplished."[36]

The might of this Word is enough to overwhelm God's enemies without any human help. It can do without any support or confirmation from men.[37]

But the proof *par excellence* of the power of God's Word is the Gospel. God does not let his Word return to him empty (cf. Isa. 55:11). Evangelical doctrine in its totality is nothing but a complete assurance that God's promises will certainly be realized. The Gospel itself is the accomplishment of the promise, for in it everything promised to the patriarchs and to the whole human race is carried out, and our own hopes are fulfilled, just as Simeon said (Luke 2:29-32).[38]

Here is the point of Zwingli's argument: The power of God's Word *is* the Gospel, the salvation of men. If the power of the Word is compared to the force of the Rhine, it is not merely to draw our attention to the energy required to move huge masses of water. Creation itself, including everything that exists, is not the whole of knowable reality. There is something other and beyond which crowns nature and gives it its meaning: man and above all man's salvation in Christ. For the man of faith, who is man as he really should be, the power of God's Word is revealed above all in what it accomplishes for him in Jesus Christ. "He who did not spare his own Son but gave him up for us all, will he not also give us all things with him?" (Rom. 8:32.) The meaning, the power, the purpose, the goal, and even the justification of God's Word is Jesus Christ.

"Nobody can resist God's Word," Zwingli wrote in his *Schlussreden*,[39] "for it is free of every earthly attachment or temptation and purer than silver or the finest gold." Those who receive it in faith are completely certain of their salvation. It is as if they were sent a sealed letter to confirm it (John 3:15, 36). On the other hand, "the man who stumbles on this stone will be broken; if the stone falls on him it will grind him to powder" (cf. Matt. 21:44, K.J.V.). Broken! Pulverized! That is the kind of power God's Word has over those who resist it. Such is the judgment that is meted out on unbelief, for unbelief is sin at its worst.[40]

The power of God's Word thus exceeds anything man can imagine, for it is the power of Christ himself: complete assurance for the believer and complete bafflement for the unbeliever. The power of God's Word points to Christ, and gains its whole meaning from him.

The Clarity of the Word of God

If the Word of God is powerful, it is also clear. It is clear because it is Jesus Christ, and because Jesus Christ is the Light. Resuming his citation of John 1:19, "The true light that enlightens every man was coming into the world," Zwingli remarks, "If the light enlightens every man, this must be because it is the very essence of clarity itself."[41]

Thus Zwingli does not say that the Word of God is clear in relation to some independent standard of clarity, as, for example, we say that a lecture is clear because we already have some idea of what clarity means. The Word of God is clear because it is lucid in and of itself. The Word of God is clear on its own terms, and not in comparison with anything else. This clarity is the clarity of faith, of revelation.

The Word of God is clear also because it has a precise purpose: to make us grasp God's intention for us. "The fact that God has taught us by parables from the beginning of the world, and that now he has made his teaching clear through Jesus Christ, is a sign of God's lovingkindness toward men."[42] Parables are enigmatic precisely to stab our spirits awake and to involve us with all our powers in God's work, which is actually accomplished on our behalf. The Word is clear because it shakes men's minds out of indolence more than any other word can. Even in parabolic form, the Word raises penetrating questions which light up the deep recesses of our being. When we ourselves pose questions for Christ or his witnesses to answer, we find that the Word becomes clearer still, to the point of being "existential," if one may say so. The parable of the Sower (Matt. 13) is a good example. Here the disciples, as it were, are seized and surrounded by the pointedness of the Word.[43] This parable, furthermore, shows us that the explanation of biblical texts is always to be found in the Bible itself. Scripture explains the meaning of Scripture.

Lucid for purposes of salvation, clear for those who come to it in faith, the Word is the very savor of life to believers. On the other hand, it is darkness and the odor of death for unbelievers. "If we do not trust the Word of God, it is a sure sign . . . that God's wrath will soon catch up with us."[44]

The clarity of God's Word, furthermore, is what gives rise to the confession of faith. "When the Word of God illumines the world, it lights up human understanding in such a way that man understands it, confesses it, and is sure about it."[45] This is an active, stirring clarity which is always moving. No one can be aware of it without proclaiming it to others immediately. "There is no rest for the believer so long as he sees that his brother is still an unbeliever."[46] For the shepherds at Bethlehem (Luke 2) the angelic message, their departure to see the Christ-child, the confession implicit in their obedience, the very clarity of God's command, were all the same. The same clarity confronted Abraham, who never doubted God's promise as he set out to sacrifice his son. Clarity like this overcomes the clarity of reason and good sense. So it was with Jacob, who said when he awoke from sleep, "Surely the Lord is in this place, and I did not know it." Where, Zwingli asks, had he previously seen or heard God?[47]

No, one cannot find truth among the doctrines propounded by men, for their clarity cannot be compared with the clarity of God's Word. As the Psalmist said, men are all liars! (Ps. 116: 11.)[48] This is why Zwingli will not let anyone set himself up as a judge of Scripture. On the contrary, he is fully willing "to let Scripture judge *him,* and if it condemns him, he is glad to be condemned, for Scripture alone is the truth."[49] So, too, to government officials: "You are not above either the Word of God or the Law; rather, the Word of God is above you"[50] (literally, "You are not judge upon the Word of God . . . but the Word of God judges you").

Zwingli sees little need for apologetics. "You people inclined to argue as if you didn't trust Scripture ought to remember that God's Word has its own clarity and its own ability to convince people."[51] Scripture does not have to be explained by any outside evidence. The very definition of the Gospel implies this: "good news from God to man concerning precisely the thing man does not know or doubts."[52] The Gospel speaks to the humble, those who know they know nothing. The Jews asked Jesus by what authority he did what he did. But the people who believed in him did not need to ask. They knew perfectly well! "The Gospel itself provides the light which lets us know it is true and makes us believe it."[53] One can make no mistake here, for God himself draws men to him. "We must let the Word of God have its own nature."[54] The Word is clear on its own account precisely so we can understand it. If we force the meaning to make it correspond to our own opinions, we are like the man who comes with a hatchet in his hand saying: If you do not agree "the hatchet will speak."[55]

One can see that for Zwingli the unforgivable sin is not to believe God's Word. "Those who have God's Spirit, who know that Christ is their salvation, who rely on the Word, do not sin.

For the only mortal sin is unbelief."[56] There is no greater blasphemy than not to trust God.[57] The more God's comfort abides in us, the less room there is for sin. If we are in distress, the only possibility we have is to run to God (Prov. 3:11; 18:10).[58]

The man who has accepted Christ's testimony can be as sure of God's veracity as if he had received a sealed letter. No man comprehends God's intentions if God has not revealed them to him. But the man who has received this revelation can have more confidence in God's Word than in all the sealed letters he could possibly possess.[59] "Against this Word, the lies and fables of the lawyers, the hypocrisies of the clerics, the wrath of the prelates, the poisons of Rome, and the fires of Mount Etna can do nothing."[60] Thus to be taught by God, and not by men, to be *theodidacti* as Zwingli said, is something which one must constantly seek in prayer.[61]

II

THE
CHRISTOLOGICAL AXIS

The preceding chapter has shown that Zwingli thinks of God's Word not in and for itself but in its movement: in the relation between God and man in Jesus Christ. The exclusive character of the Word is bound to this movement, because Jesus Christ is the only way to God. Scripture thus has authority not on its own but because of Christ. This observation suggests that christology may well be the main pillar of Zwingli's theology, the axis of his thought. We will try to document this point with passages from Zwingli's works, deliberately chosen from writings of diverse kinds.

The Sixty-Seven Theses
(Uslegen und Gründ der Schlussreden oder Artikel) 1523.

Zwingli's exposition of the sixty-seven theses he prepared for the first disputation in Zurich is one of the most important systematic writings of the Reformer. These theses were designed to promote the reformation of the church, and deal mainly with practical questions, strongly criticizing certain features of traditional church practice.[1]

It is not at all surprising that the theses, considering their purpose, are based exclusively on Scripture and thus have a christocentric character. They are divided into two parts of unequal length. The first part (theses 1 to 16) lays theological foundations; the second (theses 17 to 67) draws practical consequences for the situation of the Zurich church.

The commentary on thesis 1 makes the point that Jesus Christ guarantees the authority of Scripture and that this is confirmed in the church by the Holy Spirit. "Those who say that the Gospel has no validity without the sanction of the church are wrong and offend God." From thesis 2 onward, the whole demonstration centers on Christ, "the sum of the Gospel, the only way of salvation, so that anybody who teaches otherwise is a burglar or a thief" (theses 2 and 4). Just as there is only one Christ, so there is only one sacrifice and only one path.[2] Because Christ is the "only open door to salvation, nothing can be compared with him or set beside him."[3]

Because of the fall, Adam and his descendants are dead. We are involved in this situation because we are in Adam and Adam is in us. Under these circumstances the Gospel makes its impact, for we, who have broken the Law and are condemned by it, learn that Christ, in our place, has satisfied its requirements and has purchased life for us. Indeed, there is no other way out of this situation, for "a dead man cannot come back to life by himself."[4] Here we see God's mercy. We no longer need to pity ourselves because we are condemned to death, for Christ is our prince and our chief.[5] On the contrary, we have every reason to rejoice. This is why the Gospel is the power of God unto salvation. If there are objections, "they come solely from the fact that the Gospel is not known and trusted as it ought to be."[6] It follows from this that the sin above all sins is unbelief.[7]

Zwingli uses several expressions in speaking of Christ. He calls him "Guide and Captain," and then "Head." These terms are used in different contexts. If Zwingli uses the last in connection with the church, following St. Paul, he uses the first two with respect to "mankind," suggesting that Christ ought to be regarded not only as head of the church but also as chief of the human race. This thought is developed in subsequent writings, as well as in theses 34 to 43, which deal with the civil authority. Here one sees clearly to what, or rather to whom, Zwingli appeals in matters concerning not only the church but also the state, according to the Word of God.

Theses 8 to 16 deal with the church. Church members draw

their life from the Head, and act foolishly when they act apart from him. If the clergy, for example, are not obedient to Christ, what they say is valueless, and it is hopeless for them to look for God's mercy. But when a man listens to the Head, he grasps the will of Christ and is led by the Holy Spirit. This is why the main task of the church is to preach the Gospel.

Thus, for Zwingli, christocentrism colors all of life, and consequently all reformation of the church. This is where everything must begin.

Admonition to His Fellow Countrymen in Schwyz
(Ein göttlich vermannung an die eersamen . . . eidgenossen zu Schwyz) 1522.

Admonition to His Faithful Fellow Countrymen
(Ein trüw und ernstlich vermannung an die frommen eidgenossen) 1524.

These two treatises were sent by Zwingli, the first under his own name and the second anonymously, to his fellow countrymen of cantons still faithful to the Roman Church. His purpose was to exhort them to maintain national unity, a unity threatened not only by questions of faith but by political differences having implications for the morality and independence of the country as a whole.

"God made men out of the dust of the earth" (cf. Gen. 2:7), he wrote in the first of these treatises, "to make them humble. Earth, the mother of all, will not let her children feud or lord it over each other . . . Moreover, God ordained that all men should have the same father, Adam, for precisely the same reason." And still further, God created men in his own image so that they might live together in peace and harmony like the Father, Son, and Holy Spirit.[8] "You can see from this," Zwingli continued, "that God not only intended that peace should reign among men from the beginning but that the same aim should be served by our new birth in Christ. If our natural birth and origin are not enough to unite us, we are made one by our new birth in the Spirit, just as Paul pointed out . . . (Eph. 4:1-6). And if, as Christians, we are so potently bound together, how does it happen that we fight each other like pagans? How can foreign powers make such trouble in the Swiss Confederation, where fraternal love has always been the rule?"[9]

Reading these lines, we must remember that Zwingli is writing to his Swiss fellow citizens on a political matter. The Swiss are all baptized, to be sure, and members of the church, but Zwingli's concern here is with Switzerland as a human society. He knows full well that one can be Swiss without being a child of God, and vice versa. It follows that Zwingli holds that *all* civil relationships go to pieces without Christ. Human community is impossible without him. This is the consequence of original sin. Created to live together, men are only restored to this possibility through Christ, and this is so whether they realize it or not. Men cannot live in peace with each other if Christ is not among them, and if they do live in peace, it follows that Chrst is there, whether or not they know it.

In the second treatise (this time sent anonymously, because by 1524 Zwingli was a known partisan of the new faith) the Reformer expresses himself slightly differently but to the same effect. "You know only too well," he wrote, "what Nicholas of Flue, from Unterwald,[10] said about Switzerland: that it could be conquered only by its own self-seeking *(Eygennutz)*." Philip of Macedon, Alexander the Great's father, Zwingli added, once said that there was no fortress that could not be taken by a donkey loaded with gold.[11] Self-seeking is the most destructive sin of the Swiss because it destroys all community life. In his treatise *On True and False Religion,* Zwingli describes this as the characteristic sin of man. "Self-seeking, i.e., self-love, led Adam to follow his wife's bad advice, and this is why he was condemned." It follows that "the essence of mortal sin is precisely man's persistent affection for himself."[12]

All social evils thus originate in self-seeking. The equation is simple: Apart from God, men are at war with each other because each seeks his own personal advantage; with God, the body politic lives. "When God is not in a man's heart, there is nothing there but the man alone. And if this is so, the man has nothing else to think about but his own self-interest and whatever adds to his personal enjoyment."[13]

Now if there is a realm in which Christ's nature is diametrically opposite to that of the ordinary man, it is in this matter of self-seeking. The christological axis in Zwingli's thought can thus be discerned, like a watermark, behind these arguments, whether they apply to the church or to society as a whole.

On Divine and Human Justice
(Von göttlicher und menschlicher Gerechtigkeit) 1523.

These pages, to which we shall have to return in the chapter dealing with church and state, argue that God's justice (a perfect justice) and the justice of man (imperfect) are interdependent. The latter must be inspired by the former if it is to accomplish its purpose. Zwingli argues here that the Word of God is valid for all men as it has to dominate them,[14] believers and unbelievers, understood or not. This Word must be preached publicly, for only God's grace in Jesus Christ can rescue us from our natural inability to maintain a human society (and not merely a church) worthy of the name. "Good increases in proportion to our faith in Christ," writes Zwingli in his "Introduction to Preachers."[15] The body politic is not viable unless Christ is there, whether man knows it or not.

On True and False Religion
(De vera et falsa religione) 1525.

This treatise has been called the first Reformed dogmatics and is regarded by many Zwingli scholars as the Reformer's principal work. Here dogmatic presuppositions and ethical consequences are systematically co-ordinated. The treatise is dedicated to Francis I of France, who was at this time still held as a friend of humanism and of the infant Reformation. One of the purposes of the writing was to help win France for the Reformed cause, as Calvin was also to seek to do in dedicating his *Institutes* to the same monarch. In this particular among others, Zwingli was precursor of the Reformer of Geneva.

Religion here is treated in dynamic terms. It can only be comprehended as a constant interaction "between two poles: the object of religious devotion and the subject who worships that which lies beyond himself."[16] And because for Zwingli there is no real knowledge of God apart from Jesus Christ, one is not surprised to find that the Reformer treats these two aspects of religion in scriptural terms even when the Christian faith as such is not being considered. In other words, Zwingli works in terms of an *analogia fidei,* not an *analogia entis.*

"It is as plain as day that religion began at the moment God called wayward man to himself. Otherwise the human race would have dispensed with God entirely. Man saw that he was naked. In other words, he saw that his depravity was so severe that there was no evident possibility of recovering fellowship with God by his own powers. But God was merciful. He took compassion on the fugitive and on the soul in despair. Like a good father, who deplores the folly or the insolence of his child but cannot hate the child himself, God gently calls the doubter and the lost. He asks how life is going. 'Adam, where art thou?' Oh, the marvelous and ineffable gentleness of the heavenly Father! He, apart from whose command nothing would exist, calls, 'Adam, where art thou?' He calls for that unhappy man's sake, to show him his sin. For man no longer knew where he was. In distress, Adam saw that everything was finished for him, for his country and for his household. He acknowledged that God's Word was all too true when he said, 'In the day that you eat of it you shall die' (Gen. 2:17). He felt his heart beating with the clash of conflicting thoughts: misfortune, treason, trouble. He expected to die at any moment. That is why the heavenly Father asked, 'Adam, where art thou?' It was so that man would always remember where, when, and how God had graciously called him. So I say," wrote Zwingli, "that it was here that religion, or rather loving confidence, was born. Such things remain between parents and children."[17] Loving confidence or religion is thus defined as follows: God leads man to acknowledge his disobedience, his treason, his misery, as Adam did. "When man becomes wholly unsure of himself God opens wide his heart to him."[18]

Defining religion in this way, Zwingli certainly was thinking primarily of Christianity. But it is worth noticing that in this treatise the paragraph entitled "Concerning Religion" comes before the one entitled "Concerning the Christian Religion," and that Zwingli does not explicitly mention Christ in the former paragraph because "one cannot say everything at once."[19] Yet even in terms of the economy of creation, if one may describe the argument this way, the principal axis of Zwingli's thought shines through. The merciful God—the God who takes the initiative in calling Adam, who otherwise would have remained a fugitive and would have become his own god;[20] the God who detests sin but who cannot hate the guilty child; the God without whom man no longer knows where he is; the God who makes man aware of his predicament and convinces him that what he told him before was true (and who apart from God could do this?)—all this is comprehensible only in and through Christ. For, as Zwingli put it, "Just as God created man through his Son, so he resolved to save man through his Son." Creation and redemption are thus inseparable (John 1:3; Col. 1:16).[21]

So, for Zwingli, religion, including religion in general, gains its significance from what God did once for all in Jesus Christ. Christ was already present in God's call to man immediately after the fall. It was through Christ, indeed, that God called Adam. And if religion in general is based on God's initiative in Jesus Christ, the fulfillment of all religion is the faith which explicitly knows and acknowedges these things: the Christian faith.[22]

On the Providence of God
(Ad illustrissimum Cattorum principem Philippum sermonis de providentia dei anamnema) 1530.

This is the treatise which has led many commentators to call Zwingli fundamentally a philosopher and a rationalist. The language of the work is indeed philosophical. Zwingli appears to borrow heavily from Aristotle and the Stoics. The doctrine of

God is treated as derivative of the doctrine of being as such (*analogia entis*). But, on the other hand, it is equally true here that providence is connected with the doctrine of predestination, which shows that the treatise is essentially concerned with faith, however philosophical may be its terminology. Indeed, this is an example of the use of philosophy to serve theology, as Gottfried Locher has pointed out in his excellent book.[23] The text of Zwingli's treatise was originally a sermon preached before the Landgraf of Hesse at the time of the Marburg Colloquy in 1529.

"Man," Zwingli says, "is the most admirable of all creatures of the world . . . indeed, he surpasses the beauty of the angels. If you compared a rooster with a bull, you would find the bull mightier. But you could not but admire the rooster's royal plumage, his noble soul, his proud posture, his undeceivable vigilance, his imperious and dominating air, even if he is only leading a flock of chickens. Another thing: The angels are made of the noblest substance; they are pure spirit. But it is disconcerting to compare them with men, who are both heavenly and earthly beings. In the whole realm of the spirits there are none who clothe themselves in earthly, visible bodies (unless an angel should do so temporarily). And among all the creatures of earth, men are the only ones which have the intellectual capacity for dominating and directing creation. From this it is easy to see that God the Creator made man in his own image, not merely to provide an earthly example of the divine nature but so that man might enjoy communion with God: here in lovingkindness given and received, and later in the full realization of heaven. In the last analysis, God created man to be the prefiguration of the whole relationship between God and the world which would come into being through Christ. What better preparation for understanding the Incarnation could there be than seeing, from the very beginning, intelligence dwelling in the inherently insentient human body?"[24]

If these remarks are read out of context, one may be perplexed about what Zwingli means. Where is the beginning and where is the end? What is the point of the argument? Does one begin with a knowledge of man and deduce from this a knowledge of Christ

and of the Incarnation? Or does our knowledge of Christ lead us
to the true understanding of man? It could be said, presumably,
that man is able by his own efforts to discern the superiority of a
rooster to a bull, even though this particular conclusion is hardly
self-evident. Human intelligence might even discern that a man
is superior to an angel, although revelation could very well play
a part in a statement of this sort. But when Zwingli argues that
man is a foreshadowing (cf. Col. 2:17; Heb. 8:5; 10:1) of the relationship between God and the world in Jesus Christ, he definitely brings revelation into the discussion. Indeed this last point
explains and conditions the whole preceding demonstration. It is
because of Christ that man is on earth. It is because of Christ that
a man is superior to an angel. Indeed, if we remember that we
are dealing with a parable, it can be said that it is in the light
of Christ that Zwingli insists that a rooster is superior to a bull.
Here, it would seem, is a clue (and it would be possible to find
others) that, even in this writing, the key to Zwingli's theology is
his christology.

The sixth chapter of the treatise is called "The Election
Which Theologians Call Predestination." The presence in this
"philosophical" book of such an exclusively theological *locus* (the
predestination of which Zwingli speaks is not philosophically
conceived) forces the reader to consider the whole treatment of
God's providence in a theological framework. Zwingli's basic
analogy is still the *analogia fidei*, not the *analogia entis*. Moreover, Zwingli ought to be explained by Zwingli. A text which is
difficult to interpret at first glance ought to be compared with
earlier writings by the same author. Zwingli's earlier writings give
ample reason to believe that christology is one of the main pillars
of his thought, if not indeed its central axis. A final quotation
from the treatise on providence will show that we must not de-
viate from this christological basis if we want to grasp what the
writer means. "It may be," Zwingli writes, "that all these things
will appear superficial, or even carelessly written. But even though
I have used more rational arguments than references to Scripture,
the latter are not missing when they are essential. Indeed, Scripture is the unshakable basis of the whole demonstration."[25]

In his book on Zwingli,[26] Paul Wernle admits his perplexity concerning this treatise on providence. According to Wernle, Zwingli appears to be a rationalist who looks for biblical quotations to support his point of view. Theoretically a monist, he is a dualist in practice. Wernle sees both the philosopher and the Reformer in Zwingli, but he does not see what ties these two aspects of Zwingli's personality together. Gottfried Locher[27] is critical of this analysis. Wernle, Locher says, cannot find harmony in Zwingli's thought because he has not discovered its central axis. With Locher, we believe that christology is this center.

That elements of natural theology are to be found in Zwingli's writing no one denies. But the natural theology is, so to speak, wrapped up in the revealed theology. Elsewhere, Zwingli defines reason as that which is in conformity with God's Word, and irrationality as that which contradicts it.[28] Revealed theology is the indispensable presupposition of all philosophy worthy of the name. True philosophy derives its meaning from the revelation of God in Jesus Christ, and to this same revelation any meaningful philosophy is bound in the end to return. For Christ is the *alpha* and *omega* of all things—philosophy and theology included!

III

THE CHURCH

The Doctrine of Election

The church is based on God's promises to man. It follows from this that it is also grounded in God's election, which is the expression of his justice and his kindness.[1] The whole of what God has done is done for the welfare of man. Just as Law and Gospel are one and the same, so God's justice and God's kindness coincide in Zwingli's thought.[2] Gottfried Locher[3] has pointed out that this view is different from the position later taken by Calvin, for Calvin connects election mainly with God's majesty and authority. According to Zwingli, "it is not the merciful God who elects and the righteous God who rejects. It is the good, merciful, and righteous God who, in his wisdom, elects out of his own free will."[4] Pharaoh, who was hardened to manifest God's justice, and David, who was made a king to show forth God's kindness, are both witnesses to the same comportment of God toward the world.[5] Zwingli, moreover, seems to prefer the word "election" to the word "predestination."[6] The former term is more in harmony with God's plan for saving the world through Jesus Christ, and for incorporating mankind into his church. Locher seems to interpret Zwingli's thought correctly when he points out that election is not one decision of God among others but the whole triumph of his justice, mercy, and goodness.[7]

The elect are identified with the members of the church. Faith is the consequence of election (Rom. 9:11-13) and its surest sign. By faith, the believer seizes his election and is sure of it.[8] "Faith goes before election."[9] When Mark writes, "He who does not believe will be condemned" (Mark 16:16), he means that he who is not elected will not be saved.[10] But this sentence, says Zwingli, "is not intended for elected persons who have not yet come to the faith" (*tempestevitas fidei*).[11] What Mark says is there only for those who can understand it by grasping it in faith. It is not for anybody else.[12] The doctrine of election is incomprehensible apart from the church. It is a mystery, and it can be understood only by those who are in the church. Election, then, is a doctrine *ad usum internum;* it loses its meaning if it is considered a self-subsistent truth, or if it is applied apart from God's purpose of gathering his church in Jesus Christ. Election is grounded upon Christ's saving work. Apart from Christ, election does not exist. The doctrine of election, therefore, has meaning only for the Christian believer.

This viewpoint requires church members to view others with what Calvin later called a "judgment of charity."[13] In the absence of definite proof to the contrary (and absolute proof to the contrary is hardly possible) the Christian must consider his neighbors in principle as elected, even if they have not yet responded to their election with faith. "As long as I do not find unbelief in anyone (i.e., deliberate refusal to believe God's promises when they have been clearly heard), I have no reason to condemn him."[14] This is one reason why pagans can be saved[15] and why little children can be baptized. In principle, they are considered to be elected. Little children are not to be judged by the extent of their faith, for, as Locher puts it, God's mercy is not bound to our faith, but, on the contrary, our faith is bound to his mercy.[16] The fact that Esau lived to adulthood indicates that his unbelief had to be unmasked. If he had died as a child, it would have been assumed from this very fact that he was numbered among the elect.[17]

Yet scholars like Locher notice here that Zwingli is torn between the implications of the doctrine of election and the universalism toward which he personally leans. Is there not a warning here for theologians who apply their human standards to the doctrine of election and only succeed in erecting barriers before God's goodness, mercy, and justice? Surely there are examples of just this mistake in 17th-century Protestant orthodoxy and, to a certain extent, in the theology of Calvin.

The Jewish People

The church is one in time and space. It begins not merely with Pentecost but with Abraham. Better said, it begins with Adam and is renewed in Abraham.[18] "God has made the same covenant with us that he formerly made with the people of Israel. We ought to be one people with the Jews. We ought to have one church and one covenant in common." This does not mean we must become Jews. But "the people which honors the one true God must always be one and the same, even if it has diverse parentage. . . We were put in place of the Jews after they were pruned like useless branches. We were not merely put alongside them. If we speak of two Testaments, it is not because they are essentially different from each other. If they were, there would be two different peoples, and even two different Gods for these two different peoples. . . Paul teaches us (Rom. 11) that out of two peoples Jesus Christ raised up one. He united those who were close by, the Jews, and ourselves who were far off. . . Several other passages (Heb. 12:22; Acts 2:30; 10:34; 11:18) show that only one covenant has been made by God to last from the beginning of the world to the end. God is not inconsistent . . . he made ready the mediator, Jesus Christ the Saviour, even before Adam's fall. God has not come to the rescue of mankind with any other covenant. . . The one covenant has been made known to all peoples, and therefore God has only one people."[19] The fact that Abraham rejoiced that the time was fulfilled and that Christ had come into the world shows that the Saviour was the same for him as for us. With him, we are one people and one church.[20]

One catches here a glimpse of the cosmic dimension Zwingli gives the church, and this without the slightest concession to deism or natural theology. Not only are the Jews part of the church, but God's covenant with Abraham was the concretion of his covenant with Adam, whose center was already Jesus Christ, head of the church and Lord of world history. It follows that the

Jewish people, without knowing it, is destined to appear as such within the church. And it is impossible, therefore, to speak of the whole church without including the Jews.

Different Meanings of the Word "Church"

In his *Exposition of the Sixty-Seven Theses,* Zwingli points out that the word "church" is used in two senses. It is used, in the first place, to mean all those who are grounded and built up in faith in Jesus Christ (John 6:40) who is the cornerstone of the whole building. Those who are part of this church cannot be condemned. The church, in this sense, is the bride of Christ gathered by the Holy Spirit. But the word "church" is also used for the local communities of which Christ speaks in Matthew 18: 17, and to which Paul refers in the salutations of his epistles. Churches, in this sense, "are the great assemblies and communities in which people can gather to hear the Word of God" which we call parishes.[21]

Later, in his commentary *On True and False Religion,* Zwingli distinguishes between the total of all who claim to be Christians (as in the parable of the Dragnet, Matt. 13:47),[22] constituting the "one church called catholic by the Greeks and universal by us,"[23] and particular local communities such as those at Antioch or Corinth. The same picture can be found in Calvin's *Institutes.*[24] Thus Zwingli gives the word "church" three meanings in all: the *Una Sancta* which is the bride of Christ, the whole body of those who claim to be Christians, and the particular local community. It is only by forcing the facts that one could say that Zwingli uses the familiar schematism of visible and invisible as applied to the church, and he certainly does not use it in the sense it acquired in the nineteenth century.

The Marks of the Church

Calvin's definition of the church is familiar. "Wherever we see the Word of God purely preached and heard and the sacraments administered according to Christ's institution, there, it is not to be doubted, a church of God exists. For his promise cannot fail: 'Where two or three are gathered in my name, there am I in the midst of them' " (Matt. 18:20).[25] There are thus, according to Calvin, two marks *(notae)* of the church. These *notae* rest upon God's promise which cannot fail. God's promise is the guarantee of their quality as *notae*. Thus it follows that *notae ecclesiae* only function as such in the realm of faith. If the *notae* allow one to say with certitude where the church is to be found, they nevertheless do not permit one to say that any particular local community is a true church in every way and in every one of its members. Is there similar teaching in Zwingli's writings?

a. In his *Exposition of the Sixty-Seven Theses* Zwingli defines the church as "the whole community of those who, in one faith, are grounded upon and built up in the Lord Jesus Christ" (Article 8). Further on he adds, "here below it is gathered by the Spirit of God in one hope; in heaven it is gathered around God alone. Who knows the church? God himself!"[26] This definition, we must notice, does not imply the familiar schematism of the visible and the invisible church, but rather the idea of one church having both aspects. Moreover, the definition implies movement— from heaven to earth, from divine revelation to earthly manifestation, from faith to sight. We cannot leave this movement out of account when we deal with Zwingli's ecclesiology.

b. In the *Commentary on True and False Religion* the word "church" is used "for all who consider themselves Christians and live in a Christian context even if they really have very little faith." Thus when Paul says that he persecuted the church of God (1 Cor. 15:9) he means those who called themselves Christians.[27] Within the church, taken in this sense, the good and the evil are together, as Christ made clear in his parables of the Tares and of the Dragnet (Matt. 13), and of the Ten Virgins (Matt. 25).

But even when the church is considered as a sociological reality, its quality of churchliness comes exclusively from above, from God's promise, and not from anything which man can discern. We need not be misled by the common use of the word "church" for ecclesiastical assemblies, for what makes the sociological reality a church in the first place is what makes the church the bride of Christ, pure and undefiled. Indeed, if the church were considered *only* from this point of view, Zwingli remarks, it would not exist any more than Plato's ideal republic. But the church *does* exist on earth. Why? Because it exists not in and of itself, but by the grace of Christ (Eph. 5:25). It exists because God came to us in the Incarnation. One is even able to say that insofar as the church is founded on the Word of God it is infallible.[28]

This leads Zwingli, always thinking in terms of the movement from heaven to earth, to say that "the church is not where prelates are gathered but where people adhere to God's Word, where Christ is lived."[29] At the moment when this is the case, when God's promise is fulfilled that the sheep will hear and recognize the shepherd's voice (John 10:11-30), one can say that the church exists at a particular place. But even this statement can be made only in faith. For what one can actually see never proves that the church exists, but only constitutes a *préjugé favorable,* a favorable presumption that the church is there.

This favorable presumption applies to local communities whose members confess Jesus Christ and subject themselves to Christian discipline. "Local churches have the right to exclude scandalous sinners, and to readmit those who are penitent to the community of grace."[30] Yet discipline is not considered by Zwingli a *nota ecclesiae* in the strict sense even though it is the right and duty of every local church. In this, Zwingli differs from Bucer who tends to include discipline among the *notae* themselves.

The nature of the church is best grasped in the movement of faith, starting from Christ's promise and moving to the community of those who confess him. Intellectually speaking this is a "one way" movement, corresponding to the *analogia fidei.* It is not because there exist people who call themselves Christians that a group of them can be called a church. The church of God can never be recognized by the piety of its members,[31] but only by the fact that it is founded on Christ through faith. To the degree that the church is so founded, it exists visibly as the bride of Christ, pure and undefiled, wherever it may be. Because the church has this transcendent basis, and yet must live on earth, it must repent and be reconciled to Christ again and again.

For the church *must* live in the world. It is not merely a possibility but a necessity that the church of Jesus Christ should be visible.[32] Even though one cannot say on sociological grounds alone that any given congregation is the church, the church is certainly not present where visible manifestation is lacking. This is why the church must not only proclaim the Gospel, but also exercise discipline. It must do the latter not only with respect to sinners but also in overseeing the preaching and teaching of its pastor in the light of Scripture.[33] All this, Zwingli underlines, has to do not with the church triumphant but with the church militant in this world. "The church triumphant, so called, is something quite different and lives under wholly different conditions."[34]

c. In his *First Sermon in Berne,* on the occasion of the disputation which started the Reformation in that canton in 1528, Zwingli denies that a true church can identify itself by any particular visible sign, as, for example, the Roman Church by its hierarchy, or the Anabaptist bodies by their particular discipline.[35] For a church to identify itself in this way is to proclaim itself to be a separatist body or a sect. The words *sondere* and *besondere* used in Zwingli's original German text come from the verb *sondern,* "to separate," and make the meaning unmistakable. Over against this, the Reformer speaks in his sermon of signs of the church such as overseers and apostles who point us toward preaching, the sacraments, and discipline.

Although some things in this document seem to come near being *notae ecclesiae,* what Zwingli offers should be taken only as a series of guidelines to help us grasp properly, in faith, what God's promise implies, and to draw the practical consequences. For it is only by faith, and indeed in the risk of faith, that one can seize the reality of the church.

d. The *Fidei Ratio,* dedicated to the Emperor Charles the Fifth on the occasion of the Diet of Augsburg in 1530, seems to come one step closer to defining *notae ecclesiae* as such. Zwingli here speaks of "the believer who is sure of being among the elect because he has received the firstfruits of the Spirit" (2 Cor. 1:22), for the Spirit cannot lie. This assurance, however, is purely inward and personal. It concerns only the person in question himself, who cannot, in the nature of the case, know the spiritual state of his neighbors. The fact that individuals know themselves to be children of God is not a *nota ecclesiae*. But when Zwingli goes one step further and speaks of "those who confess Christ according to God's Word,"[36] we come close to something that *can* be considered a mark of the church. To this extent, the confession of faith itself may be a *nota ecclesiae* in Zwingli's thought.

e. The *Fidei Expositio* of 1531, a writing dedicated to King Francis I of France, was Zwingli's final theological work and to a certain extent his spiritual testament. Here the Reformer argues that although God alone knows who the members of the church are, and although in this respect the church is invisible, the members of the church, whoever they may be, are visible human beings who live on earth like everybody else.[37] If all those who outwardly confess Jesus Christ are not necessarily members of the church in the eyes of God, it is nevertheless true that all those who *are* members of the true church confess Jesus Christ without exception.

Here we come to what can legitimately be called the *nota ecclesiae* of Zwingli's thought: the act of confessing the faith. If we compare this with what Calvin subsequently says, it will be evident that the Reformers of Geneva and Zurich say approximately the same thing and understand it in the same way. Basing their views on God's gracious promise, Zwingli holds that the church exists where people confess the faith, while Calvin sees the church where God's Word is correctly preached and heard and where the sacraments are administered according to the Lord's institution. But the latter is meaningful only in terms of the promise that "where two or three are gathered together in my name, I am in the midst of them," or in other words, "where they are confessing my name." Thus the formulations of Zwingli and Calvin are different ways of expressing the same truth.

If confession of the faith by believers can be considered the

mark of the church according to Zwingli, we must never forget
that this confession still implies the dialectical movement typical
of his thought. We cannot say that a given congregation is a
church without ascending along with it in faith to him whom it
confesses. It is only in dependence upon the promise of the Lord
who is its head that a church on earth can represent itself as such.
Here, in the *analogia fidei,* there is a movement downward from
God's promise to mankind, and a movement upward to the source
of the church's being in God. Thus it is impossible to be a capi-
talist in the realm of the Spirit!

It is only through this dialectical movement of thought that we
can try to grasp what the church really is. We can never do this in
a static way, postulating on the one hand an "invisible church"
and on the other a "visible" one, supposing the first to be the
true and perfect church and the other only a sociological group-
ing. To use an expression taken from a recent book in French,[38]
the church is fundamentally *event,* and only secondarily institution. And to use a phrase which probably first appeared in the
17th century in the Netherlands, the church is *semper reformanda,*
"always subject to reformation."

The Ministry and the Ministries

If the church takes shape among those who confess Jesus
Christ, then Christ must be preached. Ministry is thus indispensable to the very existence of the church. "Just as there were
Ephors in ancient Sparta, and Tribunes in Rome, and just as
there are persons at the head of the councils of many German
towns today whose job it is to intervene if the chief of state tries
to abuse his power, so God has his office-bearers *(Amptlüt),* his
pastors, among his people, whose function is to watch constantly
over the flock."[39]

One notices the way Zwingli argues here, which suggests, at
first sight, that he uses a form of *analogia entis.* But the argument
is not that because there are magistrates in the civil state there
must be ministers in the church, but rather that because God
intended there to be ministers in his church, magistrates, by

analogy, are needed in civil affairs.[40] The organization of civil society is a reflection of God's will for his church. As Karl Barth has put it, this is an analogy of relation in which the first term is the church.

It follows that the ministry is a divine institution which belongs to the being, the *esse,* and not merely to the well-being, the *bene-esse,* of the church. Those who are entrusted with ministry must learn their office from the Word of God alone, which is spoken visibly, audibly, and clearly in Jesus Christ. They will not behave according to human doctrines, but according to the Word of which they must be the heralds, to the exclusion of every other authority. But, on the other hand, no one can be a minister who has not been appointed by the competent authorities of the church—that is to say, by the church itself. He who sets himself up as a preacher *motu proprio* dismembers the church just as much as the Anabaptists do when, contrary to Christ's command, they rebaptize people who have already been baptized in infancy. "This is how the Christian community becomes fragmented,"[41] says Zwingli. This is the road which leads straight to sectarianism.[42] A regular and official ministry is as necessary to the unity of the church as is baptism—once only administered.

Ministry is a function which the church delegates to one of its members, who then proceeds to see that the function is carried out, regardless of the manner in which the delegation has been given.[43] This is so important to Zwingli that "there is no more divine right than this: the whole congregation, whether advised by bishops or by Christians who are pious and well-informed, is entitled to choose its pastor."[44]

There are four kinds of ministry, according to Ephesians 4, each of which is a ministry in and of itself. Zwingli here speaks of *ministries,* using the plural form, and lists the ministries of the apostle, the prophet, the evangelist, and the pastor or doctor.[45] All deal with the preaching of the Word, and resemble each other so far as function is concerned with the exception that the apostle is set a little apart, because this term denotes either one of the original Twelve or one whose ministry takes him from place to place. In principle, there is an open door here to missionary activity. But like the other Reformers, Zwingli does not pass through it.

In any case, this pattern shows that if there are several ministries in Zwingli's view, this plurality is secondary to the main function which all the ministries share: the preaching of the Word. Fundamentally, thus, there is but one ministry.[46] "The ministry of the prophet, that of the bishop or pastor, and that of the evangelist constitute together one single office."[47] But Zwingli adds something here which will prove to be very important in the Reformed tradition, something which Bucer and Calvin draw out. All through his writings, Zwingli uses a particular word to describe the ministry: that of "watchman" or "overseer" (*Wächter*). "Each church needs to have a watchman or overseer to keep the mischievous goats under control, and this not by the authority of the watchman but by that of the church."[48] Alongside the functions of preaching and teaching, Zwingli thus mentions another, that of watching over the flock.

Of course, both functions may and even should in most cases be exercised by the same man. The very title "Pastor" (*Hirt*— which is also the title of one of Zwingli's books) implies both and suggests that every preacher must also be a watchman. Indeed, Zwingli sometimes speaks of "the watchman or pastor."[49] The image of the shepherd and the sheep is so descriptive both of God's relation to us and of our ministry that the Old Testament uses it throughout to convey to us the meaning of God's governance and providence.[50] The pastor, then, preaches and oversees. In large communities, however, it is perfectly conceivable that these functions might be separated, and that the office of surveillance might be carried on by someone other than the pastor, although the pastor should not have the work of oversight completely removed from his competence.[51]

Yet Zwingli's words must not be pressed too hard. The Reformer uses a great number of words interchangeably: pastor, watchman, bishop, prophet, priest, evangelist, preacher, and so on.[52] Indeed, he uses the word "watchman" also for the civil magistrate.[53]

What is important here is that the function of surveillance, in and of itself, is distinct from the function of preaching. This is a distinction which one does not find in Luther, but which appears again in Oecolampadius, Bucer, and Calvin. The theory of the four ministries is enunciated by Bucer for the first time in 1536.[54] The difference between Zwingli and Calvin in this matter is only one of degree. Bucer and Calvin merely gave precision and clarity to what Zwingli had already said. Even the word "elder" appears in the *Great Mandate on Morals* of March 26, 1530. This document, although published by the civil authorities, was undoubtedly written under Zwingli's influence. The particular expression used is interesting: "elders in the name of the congregation." This title, says Roger Ley, "indicates clearly that the elders are elected by the people and are their representatives. They are there, from the beginning, to uphold moral standards and to help combat blasphemy."[55]

Zwingli's thought thus contains a specifically Reformed element which distinguishes it from the theology of Luther and connects it with the theology of Bucer and Calvin: the principle of a plurality of ministries. In this plurality the essential elements are preaching on the one hand and pastoral oversight on the other. Both these elements of ministry are an expression of the earthly character of the church, the ministry of preaching being, of course, the first.

The ministry of oversight, in particular, leads quite naturally to the question of discipline.

Church Discipline

Although it is not a mark of the church, discipline is nonetheless an indispensable element in its existence. From the beginning of his career in Zurich, Zwingli speaks of the need for discipline as something that goes without saying. Thesis 31 of the *Sixty-Seven Theses* says that "no private person [that is, no church official acting in his private capacity] can apply the sentence of excommunication, but that the church, that is, the congregation of which the offender is a member, may do so in agreement with the watchman or pastor."[56]

This concept of discipline is based on Matthew 18:15-18 (later, Bucer and Calvin quote the same text) and to a certain extent on Matthew 16:15, which deals with the power of the keys. We say "to a certain extent" in mentioning the latter passage because Zwingli, like the other Reformers, connects the power of the keys primarily with preaching the Gospel.[57] As has been pointed out, however, the offices of preaching and oversight cannot be separated.

Discipline is applied to scandalous sinners—that is, to persons whose sin is known to the church and thus constitutes a stumbling block for others (thesis 32). One only resorts to discipline when private admonition has proved unsuccessful. This is why discipline is carried on by the church itself in conjunction with the pastor. As thesis 32 puts it, "Excommunication is the punishment for those who sin openly." In other words, Zwingli's concept of discipline has a definitely ecclesiastical character. Sin, precisely by becoming scandalous and widely known, becomes a sin against the church. Commenting on Matthew 18:15, Zwingli says that the phrase "If your brother sins against you . . ." means "If your brother sins against the church."[58] This is understandable when we remember that for Zwingli a sin against man is a sin against God, and vice versa.

Is discipline linked with the doctrine of election? It would seem not, contrary to what Pietists and Puritans were to say later, and contrary even to what one finds to a certain extent in Bucer and Theodore of Beza. If church discipline were linked with election, it would give the impression that the church on earth can in some way pass judgment on a man's eternal fate. On such an understanding excommunication would mean the exclusion of a man recognized by the church as reprobate. This viewpoint is found among some of the 16th-century Anabaptists[59] and later in the thinking of Pietist groups. To take this step is to make discipline a mark of the church *par excellence*. Zwingli, however, has quite a different opinion. Comparing Matthew 18 and 1 Corinthians 5, he remarks[60] that the church does not know the *particularis electio Dei,* which is God's own secret, but only the command: *tollite malum e medio vestri.* In excluding a sinner, the church does not mean to pronounce a judgment on his eternal fate, but only to act with a view to keeping other people from evil. Here the church acts in terms of what Zwingli calls external or human justice.[61] In these considerations one sees the great difference between the concept of discipline the Reformers intended to lay down and the way certain of their followers later misunderstood it. It is just to avoid such misunderstanding that discipline is not made a mark of the church in either Zwingli's theology or Calvin's.

For Zwingli, however severe may be the means used and whatever part may be taken by the civil authority, the purpose of discipline is to keep the church as pure as possible and to lead sinners to repent and be restored. Discipline is prophylactic treatment, a caustic medicine, as Bucer will say,[62] and above all a remedy which one hopes will cure the illness to which it is applied. This makes sense when we remember that every member of the church is regarded in principle as one of the elect even if he has not yet responded to God's call in faith. Since every baptized person is considered elected until there is proof to the contrary, there is every reason to subject him to stiff disciplinary measures which will make him think over his Christian vocation. This is why Zwingli speaks of the salutary character of the sentence of excommunication. Commenting on this, Roger Ley writes—we think correctly—that for Zwingli discipline is a form of the cure of souls, and that "if one forgets that discipline is a ministry arising out of love, it becomes simply punishment, and as such contrary to the Gospel."[63]

It is perfectly clear in all this, of course, that discipline is the business of the church only. It is a matter of record that in Zurich the civil authorities increasingly intervened in disciplinary questions as time went by. But this did not prevent Zwingli from consistently maintaining, notably in the *Amica Exegesis* and in his letter to Ambrosius Blarer, that the exercise of discipline is the exclusive responsibility of ecclesiastical authority, apart from exceptional circumstances in which the magistrate might take it into his hands. In the latter event, the magistrate would act, as at the beginning of the Reformation, in the capacity of *praecipuum membrum ecclesiae* until the church could assume its own responsibility again.[64] "I do not want anything to be decided," Zwingli wrote to Blarer, "without the agreement of the church."[65]

In sum, church discipline exists to keep the bride of Christ pure and undefiled, close to the Lord who feeds his people with his Word, at least as far as it is humanly possible to do so. Necessary as it is, discipline takes second place in the church to the preaching of the Word. But even here the dialectical movement plays its part in relating the ministries of discipline and preaching. The former derives its significance from the latter, but is not the less necessary because of that.

IV

THE SACRAMENTS

Definition

Zwingli dislikes the word "sacrament." "I wish the Germans had never let this word get into their theological vocabulary," he writes. "Some of them, when they hear it, think of something overpowering and holy which delivers the conscience from sin by its own intrinsic power. Others deny this and think of the sacrament as a sign of something holy. I could agree here if only they would not add that internal purification inevitably goes with the external use of this sign. . . And still others see the sacrament as a sign, an attestation of an inward purification, this inward purification being already accomplished."[1] It is easy to see that in these comments Zwingli is referring to Roman Catholics, Lutherans, and Anabaptists, respectively.

Zwingli's own definition of a sacrament is derived from the meaning the word had had in secular history. In antiquity, the *sacramentum* was the token laid upon the altar by men going into battle. The victor could then return and retrieve his token. The word also had the meaning of an oath, and, more specifically, an oath to the flag. The French and the Italians still observed the latter oath as a pledge of allegiance toward their chief. The connotation of something holy and sacred was unknown in the ancient world. Hence *sacramentum* is not to be treated as a translation of the very different Greek word *musterion*.

To Zwingli, a sacrament is thus a kind of induction or pledge. To receive it is to enlist in Christ's forces, and to receive in return a token, a reminder, that one must not yield but remain faithful. Against the Roman Catholics, Zwingli holds that the purpose of the sacrament is not to liberate the conscience. Only God is able to do that. It is wrong to suppose that water, oil, salt, or other elements can benefit the soul which has gone astray. Against the Lutherans, Zwingli insists that faith is a reality received by man in his heart. Faith is born when man's self-confidence is swept away and he relies exclusively on God. Of this event there can be no outward sacramental sign, for God's freedom is not bound. God vouchsafes grace when and where he pleases. So far as the Anabaptist logic is concerned, Zwingli points out that by the time the sacrament is administered the Anabaptist does not need it, for he holds it to certify something already given, and accomplished in the heart. "What good is baptism to a man who knows that God has forgiven his sins long ago?"[2]

"No, sacraments are rather signs or ceremonies . . . by which men offer themselves before the church as soldiers or disciples of Christ. The sacraments assure the church of a man's faith far more than they do the man himself. If faith is not real without a ceremonial act to certify it, it is not faith. True faith rests unshakably, solidly, and wholly upon the mercy of God, as Paul repeatedly points out."[3]

Here is something new in sacramental doctrine. The three concepts of the sacrament which Zwingli opposes lay emphasis on the individual, or at least put the individual significance of the sacrament on a level with its ecclesiastical significance. Zwingli, however, comes down strongly on the side of the church as such, and points out that the sacraments are needed more by the church than by the individual believer. The sacraments exist above all in and for the church.

There are two sacraments: baptism and the Lord's Supper. "Through one sacrament we confess Christ's name; through the other we declare that we are members of his church in remembrance of his victory. In baptism, we receive a symbol which pledges us to a new life according to Christ's teaching; in the Lord's Supper we certify that we rely upon Christ's death, participating in the joy of a community which gives thanks to the Lord who has won salvation for us on the cross."[4]

Baptism

Baptism is the sacrament through which the recipient pledges himself to a new life grounded upon the grace which is in Jesus Christ. It is the rite of repentance instituted by John the Baptist. Those who are baptized confess that they are penitents for whom life must begin over again—that they must turn their backs on their lives up to now. Baptism thus launches men on this new life. It is the introduction to it.[5]

From this standpoint, there is no difference between John's baptism and Christ's. Christ sought baptism at John's hands and was in fact baptized by John. The disciples afterward administered the same baptism to those who became Christians.[6] The fact that the disciples performed baptisms, while Christ did not, reinforces this view. It is hard to imagine that the disciples baptized others without having been baptized themselves. But who could have baptized them, if not John? The fact that Acts 19:1-10 records the rebaptism of people already baptized with John's baptism is not regarded by Zwingli as damaging to his thesis, nor is the fact that Matthew 28:19 insists on a trinitarian formula. The essential nature, the form, and the purpose of the sacrament remain the same in both these cases. John baptized unto repentance, and Christ proclaimed a message of repentance. The only difference is that John pointed to Christ, while Christ pointed to himself, and this is no difference at all for purposes of this argument. The distinction, if there was one, lay only in the method of administration. Both baptisms were instituted to make us new men. If Acts 19 mentions a rebaptism, Zwingli concludes that the first baptism was probably accompanied by defective or incomplete teaching.

John's baptism and the baptism commanded by Jesus both point to a third: the baptism of the Holy Spirit.[7] John the Baptist points this out explicitly (Luke 3:16). This is why John sends those whom he has baptized to Christ, without whom their baptism would be incomplete. Baptism by the Holy Spirit has, or appears to have, two aspects: an inward reality in which all believers participate and an outward manifestation typified, for instance, by the gift of tongues. The latter, Zwingli remarks in passing, is more a gift for others than for the speaker himself.[8] The outward manifestation of the Spirit is not indispensable, but the inward reality is quite necessary, for faith comes only by the Spirit's power.

In the church, baptism takes the place of circumcision in ancient Israel. The relationship between these two ceremonies of initiation is obvious as soon as one sees the place of the Jews in God's plan of salvation, and hence their place in the church.[9] If there is but one covenant between God and man, the purpose of the sacrament of initiation into this covenant must remain fundamentally the same even if what is taught about it changes. This is why Zwingli launches so vigorous an attack on the Anabaptists. Their rebaptism is a clear sign that they intend to create a new and different church.[10] On the contrary, baptism, like circumcision, can only be performed once. Once in the covenant, a man remains there. "The New Testament knows only one baptism. Neither Christ nor the holy apostles ever repeated it, or taught that it needed to be repeated."[11]

This analogy between baptism and circumcision, resting upon the continuity of God's covenant relationship with his people, furnishes Zwingli the basis of his argument for infant baptism. For the latter he offers scriptural arguments virtually identical with those used by the other Reformers. That church tradition and the vision of society as a *corpus christianum* had something to do with Zwingli's position is undeniable. But this fact must not be allowed to obscure the fundamental point of the argument: that the continuity and, in a manner of speaking, the identity between the covenants demand the once-for-all baptism of infants who, after all, participate in the covenant of grace like ourselves.

To be baptized in the name of the Trinity means "to be incorporated into God by faith." Baptism "is only an outward sign of the thing itself," just as when a bargain is struck the parties shake hands. This gesture is not the transmission of the purchased object but "a sign for both parties that the bargain is settled." Similarly, baptism is a visible sign, primarily for the others who are present, that the one baptized "pledges himself to a new life and will confess Christ until death."[12] Precisely because of its significance for the whole congregation, baptism has a corporate and, indeed, a churchly meaning. It is more important for the church than for the believer himself, who, after all, is already assured of his salvation by the grace of God.[13] In this sense, baptism is precisely constitutive of the church.

The Lord's Supper

Zwingli went through the most acrimonious debate of his career on the question of the Lord's Supper. It was on the interpretation of this sacrament that the projected accord between himself and Luther foundered at the Marburg Colloquy in 1529. It is thus worthwhile to dwell on the question at some length.

For Zwingli, the Lord's Supper is essentially Eucharist, thanksgiving. It is a joyful remembrance and public acknowledgment of all that Christ has done for us. Taking part in it, we openly proclaim that we are numbered among those who live on Christ's benefits. To abstain from Communion is "the summit of unbelief (*perfidia*)."[14]

The Importance of the Sixth Chapter of John

This chapter, which Zwingli adduced at Marburg in support of his position, has a fundamental place in his argument. The Jews ask Jesus, "What must we do, to be doing the work of God?" (Vs. 28.) Jesus replies, "This is the work of God, that you believe in him whom he has sent" (vs. 29). It follows that the food of which Jesus speaks in this chapter is faith. Here Zwingli sees the first mistake of those who assume that Jesus is speaking of some form of sacramental nourishment. The food in question is precisely faith in Christ. "Faith takes away all hunger and thirst. Which hunger and thirst? The hunger and thirst of the soul!" The only thing said to be necessary in this chapter is faith.[15]

In this connection, Zwingli stresses two points. Christ is our salvation because he is God and because he came down from heaven (vs. 33), not because he was born of Mary and had to die in human form. Therefore the words "bread" and "to eat" in this chapter really mean "Gospel" and "to believe."[16] Although Christ could only be offered as a sacrifice in his humanity, he can be our salvation only in his divinity. Both natures, indeed, are included in the unity of his person, but these natures need to be distinguished. It is then not Christ "eaten" (that would only be possible in connection with his human nature) but Christ killed, "sacrificed" (for in this both natures are involved), who is our salvation. When Christ says, "my flesh is food indeed" (vs. 55), he refers to the fact that his flesh is delivered to death for our salvation. It is not Christ's flesh as such which brings us salvation, but his whole person sacrificed. We are saved through Jesus' death on the cross, and not by the eating of his flesh.

Christ says, furthermore: "He who eats my flesh and drinks my blood abides in me, and I in him" (vs. 56). This sentence is spoken for the condemnation of unbelievers and for the illumination of believers.[17] It is clear that Christ is not referring to a sacramental eating, for many who eat and drink in this way are no more in God for that reason than God is in them. On the contrary, the people who abide in God and in whom God abides are those who believe that Christ's sacrifice has rescued them from sin. The bread and the manna are really the same. People die just the same after eating the latter as they do after eating the former. Fundamentally, Christ reproaches his hearers because they do not believe in him. This is why he puts his final question: "Then what if you were to see the Son of Man ascending where he was before?" The people do not understand because they do not believe. Jesus speaks in parables and images, but the unbelief of the people makes them blind and deaf. Jesus' whole point here is spiritual, for "the flesh is of no avail" (vs. 63).

It is thus quite out of the question to suppose that this passage speaks of corporeal flesh. "If Christ said that 'the flesh is of no avail,' human arrogance ought not to go on talking about eating his flesh. Will you tell me that this phrase must mean something different? That Christ's flesh cannot be 'of no avail' because we are saved from death by it? I answer that Christ's flesh avails a great deal. It avails through his death, not through our eating.

The former redeems us from death; the latter is to no purpose." [18]

"Faith, and faith alone, determines the meaning of this chapter." Faith does not tolerate our asking whether the body of Christ is truly corporeally and essentially in the sacrament. At this point human wisdom is repulsed. "The flesh is of no avail." Why are you so inquisitive? asks Zwingli. It would be better to be careful. " 'The flesh is of no avail' is a barrier of brass." [19]

The Error of Apprehension Through the Senses

Faith is based on what the Holy Spirit does in our hearts. The action of the Spirit is clear, but we do not perceive it with our senses. It is impossible to make faith dependent on what we can see, hear, or touch, with the idea of achieving religious certitude, for faith has nothing to do with what we can sense. [20] As Paul wrote, "who hopes for what he sees?" (Rom. 8:24.)

But this does not mean that Christ is not spiritually present in the Lord's Supper. For Zwingli, Christ's presence is synonymous with faith. To affirm his presence and to believe profoundly in his reconciling death are one and the same thing. The body of Christ is present for the man who puts his confidence in him, for one cannot possess Christ the Saviour apart from his body, that is to say, apart from his Incarnation. [21] If Luther had given his consent to this point, Zwingli says, there would have been no disagreement between them. And Zwingli's whole purpose was to safeguard the one thing which permits us to apprehend Christ: faith. This is the Reformer's object when he says, after recalling his interpretation of John 6, "Nothing in the Bible is absurd provided it is correctly understood through faith. If we object to your doctrine [the Lutheran doctrine] as absurd, it is because we are concerned with faith alone. . . If something is absurd from the standpoint of faith, then it is absurd indeed! There lies the kernel of the matter." [22]

Now for Zwingli it is not a peccadillo to teach that the conscience is fortified by the carnal eating of Christ's body, or to hold that sins are forgiven this way. This is nothing less than idolatry. No, "to believe that eating Christ's flesh strengthens the conscience simply leads to the loss of faith altogether, for such a belief is not supported by the Word of God. On the other hand, he who believes in Christ is neither hungry nor thirsty."[23] Zwingli's criticism of both Roman Catholics and Lutherans is that by their doctrine of the corporeal, material presence of Christ in the bread, whether in terms of transubstantiation or consubstantiation, they try to "economize" on faith. And this is an economy which puts one's salvation in danger.

The Importance of the Ascension

The Ascension of Christ plays a considerable role in Zwingli's eucharistic doctrine. One notices this, for example, in a pamphlet addressed to Luther in 1527 entitled the *Amica Exegesis*. Here Zwingli argues that the Ascension completely rules out Christ's material presence in the Communion bread. Mark 16:19, in which we read that "Jesus was taken up into heaven and sat down at the right hand of God," has to do with Christ's human nature. How could Christ's divine nature be "taken up into heaven"? "The LORD's throne is in heaven," says the Psalmist (Ps. 11:4). Christ was enthroned in heaven not only before he ascended there in his human nature but even before he was born as a man. As man, Christ was welcomed in heaven at the Ascension—in the very heaven which, as God, he had never left.[24] "He sits at the right hand of God. . . In other words, it is *there* that he finds himself, that he lives, that he rejoices and cheers the brethren that he welcomes. His being is localized so that he is only in one place at one time. . . So as not to argue for anything without a strong scriptural basis, the point that as a man Christ is circumscribed and can only be in one place at a given moment may be demonstrated as follows. In several passages of Scripture, Christ has localized himself . . . above all in the act of leaving his disciples and bodily ascending into heaven. No philosopher could make the point clearer. Furthermore, Christ announced where he would be until the last judgment. Never did he give us to understand that he would be anywhere else but at the right hand of God. We are hardly being pious if we look for Christ elsewhere than in the place where he said he could be found. We claim that Christ, seated at the right hand of God in his human nature, is at and within the very place where the infinite God welcomes intelligent creatures such as angels and men, localized as these creatures are."[25]

This is why Jesus Christ, in his human nature, cannot possibly be in heaven *and* in the eucharistic bread at the same time. It is irrelevant to look for him where he is not. Present in his divine nature both in heaven and on earth, Christ in his human nature is in heaven alone. This is a point which Calvin later argues against Luther.[26] It is worth noticing what great assurance this position gives the believer. The Christian knows that his Redeemer is in heaven perpetually, and thus out of reach of Satan's attacks. This confirms that the victory over Satan is definitive and permanent.

In his last treatise, the *Expositio Christianae Fidei* of 1531, Zwingli returns to this topic. "In the Lord's Supper, the natural body of Christ, in which he suffered on earth and in which he sits at the right hand of God, is not eaten in a material sense, but only spiritually. It is not only trifling and stupid but also impious and offensive to teach, as the papists do, that we eat Christ's body in all its peculiarities, the body in which he was born, suffered, and died. It is certain, indeed, that Christ took on a true humanity, composed of soul and body, like our own humanity apart from the tendency to sin. His body has every characteristic that any human body has. What Christ assumed for mankind's sake comes entirely from man, for he had to be entirely one of us. From this, two things follow: Christ's body possesses the same properties that our bodies do, and, secondly, whatever is bodily about Christ is our own as well. If Christ's body had corporeal characteristics which other men lack, that would give the impression that he did not take on bodily form for man's sake. Now it is only because of man's corporeal nature that he can participate in eternal life. This is why Paul . . . argues for our resurrection on the basis of Christ's and for Christ's resurrection on the basis of ours (1 Cor. 15). Starting from this very point, Augustine, that giant among theologians, concludes that Christ's body must be in a specific place precisely because it is a real body. . .

It follows, therefore, that Christ's body cannot be at several places at one time any more than our own bodies can be."[27]

One notices here, of course, that Zwingli, like Calvin, argues in terms of a realist doctrine of substance which precludes the possibility of an object's being in two places at once. But the significant theological point is the conclusion he draws in the *Fidei Ratio* of 1530. In this work Zwingli points out that by seeking Christ's humanity only in heaven and not in the eucharistic bread he avoids the heresy of "the papists and others [Lutherans] who look back to the flesh-pots of Egypt."[28] Here, again, Zwingli is arguing, according to the *analogia fidei*, against those who seek the body of Christ in or with the bread because they feel they need support in what they can see with their senses. Does Zwingli think like a philosopher here? Perhaps. But it cannot be denied that the role of philosophy here is to support the *sola fide*, and to draw attention to it exclusively.

Moreover, Zwingli has a strong feeling here that he is saying something new. A little like Luther before the Diet of Worms, he cries, "I testify before God Almighty, Father, Son, and Holy Ghost, who searches the hearts of men, that I say all this for truth's sake. I know the insatiable pride of the old Adam. . . I could have had ample occasion to satisfy it."[29] But the Reformer stands fast upon what he believes to be the true meaning of Christ's words, for it is through faith alone and not through the senses or by philosophical reasoning that these words are to be understood.

The Significance of the Sacrament

Zwingli rejects the suggestion of Carlstadt[30] that in the phrase "This is my body" Christ refers not to the bread but to himself, for it is his own body and not the bread which is given for our sake. It is true, Zwingli says, that such an interpretation might be based on John 6:51, where Jesus says, ". . . the bread which I shall give for the life of the world is my flesh." But if Carlstadt were right, the rest of what is done and said at the Last Supper would be superfluous. Jesus might just as well have said, "Eat and be happy." What, on this view, would be the significance of the words "He blessed, gave thanks, and broke it"? One either ignores the words and the actions of Christ, which is unbelief, or admits that "This is my body" refers to the bread. This means that Christ's gift to us is his body under the form of a symbol.

The real problem of the passage, therefore, rests not with the word "this" but with the word "is." "Is" here must be synonymous with "signifies." This interpretation Zwingli derived from a letter written by Cornelius Honius,[31] a letter which marked a turning point in the Reformer's concept of the Eucharist. Zwingli believed that similar views had been advanced by Wycliffe and the Waldensians, but modern research suggests that this was not exactly the case. Scrutinizing the account of the Last Supper in Luke, Zwingli argues that the sense is as follows: "This bread, which I am giving you to eat, is a symbol of my body which is delivered to death for your sakes." The words "Do this in remembrance of me" indicate that the bread is to be eaten in Christ's memory, just as if the Lord has said, "What I am giving you to eat is a symbol of my body which is given for you; what I am doing now you must repeat afterward as a memorial."

In this act, bread and wine are the symbols, not the meal. But, contrariwise, the meal as a whole is the memorial, not the bread and wine. So far as the forgiveness of sins is concerned, it is vouchsafed by the death of Christ and not by this meal in particular. Yet when this supper in Christ's memory is celebrated, the believer proclaims the Lord's death until he comes (1 Cor. 11:26). What can this proclaiming mean if not rejoicing and praising the Lord, as Christians are invited to do? (1 Peter 2:9.) This is why, in Greek, the whole meal is called the Eucharist, the "thanksgiving."[32]

Concerning the cup, or, more precisely, concerning the wine, we are told that it is the new covenant in Christ's blood. The power of this covenant comes exclusively from Christ's death, and hence from his blood. The word "covenant" or "testament" here really means the symbol of the covenant, just as one sometimes says of letters that they bear witness even though they do not breathe or speak but are signs of words that were once spoken, and acted out, by someone. Here Zwingli adds, following Hebrews

9:16, that a testament is valid only when its author has died. Christ's testament only becomes effective when his death is proclaimed. It is only at this moment that his heirs can take possession of their heritage. That the cup must be understood in this way is clearly indicated by the words "This cup is the new covenant in my blood" (1 Cor. 11:25).[33] The cup, therefore, is a symbol of the covenant just as the bread is a symbol of the body. And because the power of both resides in Christ's atoning death, men participate in the sacrament only through faith.

This, in brief, is the way Zwingli uses the word "symbol" in connection with the sacramental elements. But the term must be given its full meaning. The eucharistic bread is not a symbol of just anything. It is a symbol of Christ's body sacrificed on the cross. Zwingli does not believe that salvation can be had apart from Christ's particular sacrifice. There is nothing here that can label him an ancestor of theological "liberalism." If taking part in the Lord's Supper has any meaning at all, it means that the participants believe that their salvation depends exclusively on Christ's death. Furthermore, when the bread and wine are involved in the sacred meal, they are no longer simply "ordinary" bread and wine, even though, materially speaking, they remain so. "The celebration of the Lord's Supper in all its dignity gives the bread such a nobility that it is no longer like any other bread."[34] Because the bread and wine are symbols of the loving-kindness (amicitia) of him who reconciled mankind to himself through his Son, they must no longer be seen in terms of the matter of which they are composed but in terms of the great things they mean. For this reason, we are no longer dealing with common bread but with sacred bread. This bread, indeed, is no longer called "bread," but "the body of Christ." It is this transaction, says Zwingli, which the church came in time to call "sacramental."[35]

The Sacrament of the Church

This brings us to Zwingli's treatment of 1 Corinthians 10:16-22 in the De vera et falsa religione. When Paul writes, "The cup of blessing which we bless, is it not a participation in the blood of Christ?" he surely means that those who partake are sharing the blood of the *covenant*. And when Paul continues, "The bread which we break, is it not a participation in the body of Christ?" he means that "We bear witness to each other that we are among those who believe in Christ and are thus members of his body."[36] The word "body" here simply means "church."

Earlier, in his *Letter to Matthew Alber (Ad Matthaeum Alber de coena dominica epistola)* in 1524, Zwingli put the matter similarly. "Paul clearly says that to eat this bread and drink this cup is to join our Christian brothers in one body. This is the body of Christ, because it is made up of those who believe in Christ's sacrifice for their salvation."[37] And since this communion is not merely in bread and wine, but in body and blood,[38] the sacrament is a witness borne by Christians to each other, and which they bear together to Christ, "so that each brother can see how the others have bound themselves to him in one body, one bread, and one confession, just as if they had sworn an oath, whence the term 'sacrament.' "[39] Why is this sacramental meal necessary? Because each Christian must make it clear to other Christians that he is a member of the body of Christ and each Christian must know that the others are members of the body, too.

This is why, among other reasons, Christ gave us bread. In eating it we join ourselves together in one body, his own body. We have, of course, already eaten the "heavenly bread" (cf. John 6:51). We are already believers. "This body," says Zwingli, "is Christ's church, and that is why to the extent that we are in this body we are called 'bread.' In eating this bread we confess before our brothers that we are members of Christ's body."[40] Here Zwingli clearly makes the Lord's Supper constitutive of the visible church and does so in such a way that the necessity of the Supper could hardly be rendered more evident. The Eucharist is indispensable to the church as such, and to the believer in his relation to the church—not *primarily* to the believer as an individual.

Julius Schweizer, in his book on this subject,[41] has reached similar conclusions about Zwingli's position on the basis of the Reformer's proposed liturgy for Holy Communion *(Aktion und Brauch des Nachtmahls,* 1525), a liturgy which was never put into practice because the civil authorities refused permission. Schweizer calls attention to the simplicity of the furnishings, to the fact that the holy table is no longer in the choir of the cathedral but in the midst of the congregation, to the fact that the officiating pastors are with the people in the nave. Antiphonal responses by men and women are inserted in the service for variety, says Schweizer; we would rather suggest that this is done to symbolize the total human character, including both sexes, of the assembled congregation. Although these people are gathered in the Grossmünster by order of the civil authorities of Zurich, they *become* the body of Christ, their Lord. "Through the action of the Holy Spirit in the sermon which is part of the service, the congregation undergoes transubstantiation, not symbolically but *realiter*. The community of Zurich Christians becomes *verum corpus Christi*." It is for this that Zwingli "gives thanks."[42] It is his body "which Christ, through the Holy Spirit, seeks to assure of his presence, and to draw to him in his lovingkindness."[43]

Is there, indeed, a transubstantiation of the gathered community into the body of Christ? This is surely the meaning of the congregational prayer included in Zwingli's liturgy. "O Lord . . . who by thy Spirit has made us one body, thine own, in the unity of faith. . ." In response to this act of Christ, the community gives thanks, whence the term "Eucharist."[44] Schweizer remarks that there is here a veritable transposition of the Mass into Reformed categories. Transubstantiation no longer concerns the bread, but the whole congregation, and it is *this* "body of Christ" which the congregation offers in oblation to its Lord. The body, then, is not localized in the bread but in the church gathered about the bread. Precisely here is the doctrine of the real presence in Zwingli's theology.

There is no need to stress the importance of this conclusion. One need only add that two things need to be distinguished here. On the one hand there is forgiveness of sins, grounded in God's all-sufficient mercy and received in faith. On the other hand there is membership in the church, in which one is ingrafted into a body of those who are saved, a fact attested by the celebration of the sacrament which in this connection is indispensable.

But to distinguish these things is not to separate them, for they are inevitably linked. The word "church," we remember, means in Zwingli's thought both the *Una Sancta,* the bride of Christ, and the local community, the parish. The two are dialectically linked. The sacrament is especially connected with the church in the local sense, yet this means that it is connected with the church in the full meaning of the word as well. From such a concept, all individualism is necessarily excluded. The sacrament is only the sacrament if it is the sacrament *of the church.*

This "ecclesial" setting offers the only proper background for understanding Zwingli's idea of the eucharistic memorial. It corresponds, of course, to the "ecclesial" dimension which informs his theology as a whole. Here Zwingli says something new in the history of Christian thought which does not seem to have been taken up by the other Reformers. Those who give thanks for the Lord's gift of salvation do so together. Together they confess their faith, for this corresponds to God's will for humankind. To be more precise, this proclamation of the death of the Lord until he comes *cannot be done otherwise than together.* It must be done by members of the one body, acting as such. Those who believe in Christ and are saved by him are not saved for themselves alone. They are necessarily a body.

Zwingli's eucharistic doctrine has often been depreciated as something poor and colorless in comparison with that of the other Reformers. Even Calvin downgraded the theology of the Reformer of Zurich. But we are led to conclude that such a judgment can only be the result of extremely superficial study of Zwingli's writings, if not of outright dependence on secondary sources to the exclusion of any acquaintance at all with the primary texts.[45] In particular, those who call Zwingli's conception of the Eucharist shallow tend quite unjustly to set aside the ecclesial element in the Reformer's thought, taking his concept of the Supper in a purely individualistic sense. This is, quite simply, to betray him. If there is a Reformer whose thinking about the church is particularly well developed, it is Zwingli, and this stress has its effect on his treatment of virtually every other Christian doctrine.

Church Discipline

This study has already dealt with the question of discipline, but it is well to note that it has major importance in connection with the Lord's Supper. In his letter to Matthew Alber, Zwingli remarks that participation in the body of Christ, as it is manifested in the Supper, "commits you to the Christian life in a way that exposes you to exclusion by your fellow Christians if you sin and do not repent."[46] Anyone who participates in the sacrament bears witness to his neighbor and to the church that he intends to live according to Christ's will, to live, indeed, as Christ himself did (cf. 1 John 2:6). If he does not behave in this way, he excludes himself from the church, and other Christians ought to avoid him, that is, "excommunicate" him. Here discipline, according to Christ's command, is directly related to the very being of the church whose earthly manifestation reaches its crowning point in the Lord's Supper. And it is worth repeating: This discipline must be church discipline, or it ought not to exist at all.

V

CHURCH AND STATE

The terms "church" and "state" as we use them today do not apply very accurately to the situation that existed in the 16th century. At that time there still existed a single, unified, Christian society, the so-called *corpus christianum*, of which minister and magistrate were expressions in equal measure, even if each had his own particular functions to perform. We use the terms "church" and "state" in this chapter in senses appropriate to Zwingli's epoch. It will be helpful to remember in what follows that these words need not mean exactly what they do in contemporary life.

Historians of Christian thought have often accused Zwingli of confusing the notions of church and state, and, indeed, of absorbing the church within the state. It is a fact that between 1523 and 1531, as Zwingli approached the end of his career, the state of Zurich intervened in church affairs increasingly often, particularly in the realm of discipline. To be fair, however, one must note that after 1525 Zwingli himself was in the position of a "prophet" within the Secret Council: that is, he was the authorized interpreter of Scriptures for the authorities. Zwingli's influence was such that it is hard to tell now whether, in this "Christian state," the state dominated the church or the church dominated the state. However it was, one thing remains certain: To the end of his life, Zwingli always drew a distinction between these realms, and insisted on the inalienable rights of the church as such.[1] If we are inclined to think that Calvin had greater success in this area, we ought not to underestimate Zwingli's own fundamental contribution. Zwingli was a Reformer of the first generation. He had only ten years in which to do his work. Calvin was a second generation Reformer whose active career spanned some thirty-five relatively peaceful years.

The Problem

We begin by recalling the theological basis outlined in an earlier chapter.[2] Created to live together in harmony, men are at odds with each other because of sin. God has therefore begun his creation again in Jesus Christ, the second Adam, in order that mankind may live in peace. If two men are in concord rather than conflict, if society or civilization exists at all, it is because Christ is acting among men. This is true both before the Incarnation and after. It is true whether men know it or not. Christ is therefore the basis of all human life, social or individual, for only conformity with his commands (as, for example, in the Sermon on the Mount) makes life possible.[3]

But unfortunately the real situation is a denial of this ideal. Christ's requirements, which Zwingli sums up as "divine justice," are too difficult for men to fulfill. As sinner, man is no longer capable of this "justice." To forgive one's neighbor, to offer the right cheek when one is struck on the left, to lend without hope of repayment, to love one's enemies—all these things are impossible under present circumstances even though such commandments are given for purposes of our salvation. Despite our inability to carry them out, these commandments are *still* the means of salvation because they are accomplished in Jesus Christ, on our account and in our place.[4] This is true to such an extent that, although we doubt our capacity to do what God wills, we ought to doubt no longer because of him who bore our burdens and our sins, and, by reconciling us with God, reconciled us with each other. This is why human society is viable only if Christ plays his role in it, whether men know it or not. Relying on the grace of God alone, and maintained by it, we ought to recognize that God's Word is the sole source of good. We ought to know that God's commandments, although we cannot live by them, are carried out for us in Christ, and that therefore God considers us righteous. This, indeed, is why the world goes on.

God's commands are therefore bearers of both individual and social salvation for whoever may believe. Thus, fundamentally, there is no difference between the requirements they lay down and the forgiveness they offer. "I consider as Gospel," says Zwingli, "everything that God reveals to man and everything that he requires of him," for when God requires something of us it is to save us. All that God says and does is for purposes of salvation. This is why "I am more willing to call these things Gospel than to call them Law, for they are better described from the believer's point of view than from the standpoint of the unbeliever."[5]

The Two Kinds of Justice

This is the framework within which Zwingli, in his treatise *On Divine and Human Justice (Von göttlicher und menschlicher Gerechtigkeit,* 1523), posits two sorts of justice. The first has to do with the inward man; Zwingli also calls this "the law of nature."[6] Zwingli uses the latter expression often, and in a sense quite different from that usually given it today. He comments, "It seems to me that it is none other than the Spirit of God."[7] So far as content is concerned, this law is well summed up in the Golden Rule (Matt. 7:12) and in Jesus' summary of the Law[8] (Matt. 22:37-39). The law of nature is thus "the very leadership of the Holy Spirit and his conduct of our lives" (cf. Rom. 2:14). It is then out of the question to appreciate (i.e., to believe) this law from our natural intelligence, for that we derive from Adam, and not from God the creator of all things. . . Only the believer recognizes and comprehends the law of nature. No one comes to God if God does not call him, and it follows from this that the law of nature must come exclusively from God himself.[9] It is worth noting that Zwingli finds no support in Romans 2 for what we today call "natural theology."

The law of which Zwingli speaks has been given its true meaning by Christ. Christ has "made the Law sweet" with his love.[10] Further precepts, moreover, are connected with it: Do not be angry; give to him who asks; do not covet what belongs to your neighbor; let your words imply a clear "yes" or "no"; love your enemies. Sufficient for every eventuality, this Law carries salvation with it and makes for peace among men according to God's plan. If the Law were kept by everyone, human society would be perfect. But by such standards, no one is righteous apart from Christ himself. Since the Law is not kept, and in fact cannot be because we live in sin, there must be another level of justice alongside it.[11]

This second kind of justice has exclusively to do with man in his outward actions, and Zwingli calls it "human justice." It is exemplified by such commandments as: Thou shall not kill; thou shall not steal; thou shall not commit adultery; give to every man his due. This kind of justice is of a lower order because neither can it bring us salvation nor can its accomplishment open for us the Kingdom of God. A man may be innocent by the standards of human justice, yet guilty by the standards of divine justice. A man who does not steal but yet covets his neighbor's possessions will be beyond reproach on the level of human justice, but hardly so on the level of divine. This human justice, in Zwingli's opinion, is "poor and weak," for it is not good to be considered righteous by men but not by God. It may well be that the man who covets is further from salvation than the man who, in moments of weakness, has robbed his neighbor once or twice.[12] Yet, this "poor" standard is indispensable so long as men do not practice the justice that is divine. In comparison with divine justice, human justice seems hardly worthy of the name, but yet it bears the name by right because it, too, is instituted by God and must be observed by all, believers included. Both forms of justice, indeed, depend on Christ, through whose power the world persists and history continues to unfold.

Zwingli uses a parable which will help us see the relation between the two kinds of justice. The father who turns his son over to the schoolmaster tells the latter, "Teach him this and that and don't spare the rod."[13] What does this mean? The father obviously doesn't think that the schoolmaster's main job is to whip his son, but, knowing the boy, he realizes that he will not learn much without a certain amount of coercion. So it is with such commands as "You shall not steal," or "You shall not commit adultery." If we truly loved our neighbors, commands like these would not be necessary, for love would wipe out of our hearts any idea of stealing, killing, or adultery. If divine justice were practiced, human justice would be unnecessary. But since we do not in fact love our neighbors, the thief must be made aware that he is breaking the law, and that he must give back five times what he stole. Punishment, indeed, is a reminder not only to the guilty party but to everyone else as well. The schoolmaster must keep his stick where it can be seen, and use it if necessary. The schoolmaster in this respect is just like the civil authorities.[14] Human justice is a makeshift affair, but it is a makeshift which God wills, for it is necessary in human affairs. Without it, there would be no restraint on human wickedness and "human society would look exactly like the society of irrational wild beasts."[15] Because this is the situation, governors and judges are properly called God's servants or ministers.

Another example: God forbids us to take oaths and commands us to make our "yes" mean "yes" and our "no" mean "no" (Matt. 5:37). Now we are inclined to tell lies where our own personal interest is concerned, to such an extent that any society founded on the principle that a man's word is always to be accepted without any guarantee but his own sincerity would soon be in a state of anarchy. God thus requires us to bind ourselves by oaths (to swear means to call upon God as a witness, Exod. 22:11) of a kind that if we break them the schoolmaster is there with his rod to chastise us, as God did with the two old men who wished harm on Suzannah.[16] Perjury is nothing less than a denial of God, and God has commanded that it be punished by stoning (Deut. 17:5).

So the civil authorities, on God's command, take certain measures to make sure that what men say is true, or at least take every possible precaution. They use the rod when they discover lies, because truth needs to be sought out and untruths need to be exposed if the social order is to be maintained. As Paul puts it, the government has no power over wicked thoughts, but it certainly does over wicked deeds (Rom. 13). Justice of this kind certainly is "poor and weak,"[17] because it has no way of getting at the *source* of evil actions, but it is nevertheless necessary if only to inhibit antisocial conduct. It might appear that this makes the function of human justice negative, but this is not really so. After all, the oath to tell the truth has to be taken by every citizen, whether he is good or wicked. Human justice protects the good man precisely by punishing the evil one. In doing this, it serves God. Although life in human society does not measure up to the requirements of divine justice, God nonetheless wants man to live at peace with his neighbor. This is why we are asked to pray for the civil authorities: "that we may lead a quiet and peaceable life" (1 Tim. 2:2). The duty of government is to protect the weak by bridling the wild appetites of "stubborn rams."

Because they are entitled to punish the wicked in proportion to their misdeeds, the civil authorities hold the power of the sword (the schoolmaster's rod). Yet the believing Christian ought to obey the laws for conscience' sake and not for fear of punishment, just as the good schoolboy learns because he knows it is for his own benefit and not because he is afraid of being whipped. The believer knows he has nothing to fear from the authorities. His submission, indeed, is out of obedience to God. God teaches him to love his neighbor for reasons lying in a realm to which government cannot penetrate, the realm of conscience and faith. The believer knows profoundly what he is doing when he obeys the government. He is obedient not because of the authorities but because he knows God's will.

And if the authorities are bad themselves? The Christian still has a duty to submit, because God sends such governors to chastise men for their sins. This is true even if the oppressors are childish, feeble-minded, or attended by a court like "a band of decked-out women."[18] Yet if such rulers go too far, if they attack God's Word, or order preachers to distort the Word for their particular benefit, then it is necessary to resist them, and, if needful, to depose them, for "we must obey God rather than men" (Acts 5:29). The issue to be decided here is a very serious one. "If you are not courageous enough to risk or even suffer death to change the *status quo,* then you have to endure the tyrant and possibly be struck down *with* him, for God's chastisement always threatens an evil ruler."[19]

Resistance to rulers out of obedience to God must never involve murder, war, or rebellion (1 Cor. 7:15). There are other possibilities open. If a tyrant has gained power by vote of the people, then he must be removed in the same way. If he has been put in office by princes, then the matter must be laid before these princes so that they will divest him of his charge. It is obviously dangerous to take such a way, but "it is highly comforting to die for justice' sake."[20] If the oppressor has inherited his kingdom, it is much more complicated. Yet Zwingli cannot see how anyone could inherit a kingdom without at least the implication of popular consent. In this case, no individual should take it upon himself to foment a revolt, but the whole people, or a large majority of the population, should rise up and depose the tyrant. (It is admittedly hard to see how this could be done without outright rebellion.) God would then have acted. If the children of Israel had deposed Manasseh (2 Kings 21), God would not have punished them.[21] One must pluck out the eye that causes one to stumble.

Is all this more than theoretical? Does Zwingli recommend these considerations as the basis of practical policy? It is clear that to remove a tyrant the people have to be united. If they are not united, they must put up with the tyrant and even risk being punished by God with him. Now unity and therefore the very possibility of political action are the fruit of faith and just dealings. The only way forward is for faith and justice to become more prevalent. When tyranny gets a grip on a nation, says Zwingli, "what is lacking is not the means for overthrowing the oppressor, but piety itself!"[22]

The Reciprocal Roles of Minister and Magistrate

While the civil authorities have the right to use force, and the means at their disposal to do so, Christian ministers have no power apart from the Word of God. Ministers are simply servants, messengers of Christ, stewards of God's mysteries. While they have to keep peace in the church they have no right to try to dominate it.[23] A bishop, after all, is nothing but a "watchman." The power which the clergy has usurped ought to be taken away and handed over to the civil government, to which ministers must be subject like everyone else.[24] Just as Christ did not act as a judge during his earthly life, reserving the exercise of that power until the last day (John 5:22), ministers must not act as judges either. Their duty is to teach the Gospel of righteousness and justice,[25] if necessary at the cost of their own lives, and without any fear of being called heretics, wretches, or rebels after they are dead.[26]

Since the office of a minister is to preach the Gospel, he must certainly render to God the things that are God's, but this does not dispense him from rendering to Caesar the things that are Caesar's (Matt. 22:21). Far from trying to take over the power of government, ministers must give a good example of obedience, remembering that government has its ultimate origin in God also. But in the midst of this, the minister has the positive duty of preaching divine justice to governors and people alike, remembering that it is better to lose everything than to be distracted from this task. Christ commanded us first to seek the Kingdom of God and its righteousness, and promised that everything else would be ours as well (Matt. 6:33). Only the constant preaching of divine justice, indeed, can give true meaning to human justice. If this preaching were to cease, human justice would collapse, for its only justification lies in the existence of a divine standard, apart from it and above it, which reminds men that it is not enough not to kill or steal; it is necessary to love one's neighbor as oneself.[27]

For his part, the magistrate too "derives his authority and power from Christ's life and teaching" (Matt. 22:21; Luke 2:4; Matt. 17:24-27), for Christ himself was obedient to earthly governors. Indeed, the magistrate here finds assurance that he *can* carry out his official duties. "No civil authority need fear that Christ's teaching will be an obstacle to it. On the contrary, the magistrate will soon see that his duties are never better, more peacefully, and more completely carried out than when the Word of God is being strongly and clearly preached."[28] "No doctrine is more favorable to the exercise of secular authority, or more adequate as a basis for it, than the doctrine of Christ."[29]

The governor must then act according to Christ's rule. He is not the author of this rule. On the contrary, he must be led by it. This implies that the laws must not be "against God." For practical purposes this means two things. First, the magistrate must not try to change, or improve upon, God's commandments. "You are too much a child for that. You do not judge the Word of God; the Word judges you." Second, the magistrate must use the sword to cut off the rotten members of the body politic and to protect the good. He must be careful not to cut off a healthy limb while allowing an unhealthy one to persist.[30] Furthermore, the governor must remember that he uses force in his official capacity, and not as a private person. He must be on guard against condemning men out of personal resentment, for if he does he immediately is subject to the command "You shall not kill." As a private individual, the magistrate must forgive "seventy times seven." If, on the other hand, he condemns a man to death while acting in his official capacity, he does not bear the responsibility for this personally. The responsibility then rests on the culprit, whose public offense has compelled the civil authority to deal with him as it does to prevent the evil from being propagated. But even in doing this it is well for the magistrate to remember that "if there is any hope that the guilty man may mend his ways one must give God's grace a chance to act." It is only if the case is hopeless that the criminal ought to be removed from human society (Deut. 13:5).[31]

A magistrate will have to give account of his administration before God. His office, indeed, is described by the same German word, *Amt*, that is used to speak of the ministries of the church. Zwingli holds that the magistrate is "the servant and administrator of a spiritual office *(Geistliches Amt)* before God,"[32] even when he is collecting taxes or restraining disorder by force. The Reformer even speaks of an office, or ministry, of the sword. One is tempted to ask, at this point, why God did not go the whole way and set up "an authority who could see into men's hearts and deal in terms of pure justice," punishing wickedness, so to speak, at its source. Would not human society be more just as a result? In his discussion of thesis 39 of the *Sixty-Seven Theses,* Zwingli answers, "No, for man is not God." God alone plumbs human hearts. We only know the outward actions of men, and we are able to act only when we have seen these actions. But it is still true that a judge must be a Christian believer if he is to judge justly.

A judge must know the civil laws thoroughly, and he must constantly keep in mind their relation to God's law. "This way, his decisions will be in agreement with God's will—not completely, it is true, but at least reflecting it." The justice meted out by an earthly judge can only be a shadow of God's justice, but by grace it *can* be this.[33]

But for the judges to know the laws and to apply them like believers is still not enough. The populace must be obedient and have a sense of right and wrong. "The authorities have a primary duty to see that the people acquire a proper knowledge of God," for to obey the civil laws fully is to obey them for conscience' sake. But because man is sinful by nature, God must draw man to him. "How is this possible if man knows nothing about God?" Zwingli gives a clear answer: "Where the Word of God is most clearly preached, there the law is most faithfully observed." There is no society more peaceful and God-fearing than the society in which God's Word is openly and faithfully proclaimed. "The more fully a government believes, the more stable it is."[34]

The Ultimate Purpose of Human Justice

Now we reach the climax of the Reformer's thought. After all, what is the fundamental purpose of human justice? To guarantee men a certain minimum of peaceful existence in a society which protects the law-abiding and the weak and punishes the criminal? But peaceful existence is not an end in itself. It is a transitory state on the way to something better. It is the situation in which the Gospel can be freely preached, in which salvation as the ultimate goal of human life can be proclaimed to all and received by all. The life which human justice affords is not the eternal life we are promised, but it makes it possible for men to hear about this eternal life. Anarchy, tyranny, disorder, and social injustice are not conditions favorable to the proclamation of the law of love and to the growth of faith. Although he is not

called to be a preacher, the magistrate is a fellow-worker with
God in bringing about that state of affairs in which the ministers
of the church will be able to do their specific duty of leading men
to him who plumbs their hearts, forgives, and saves them. A
magistrate who is a believer and who really knows his own duty
will require the ministers of the church to do *their* duty of proclaiming divine justice, for divine justice is the *raison d'être* of
the human justice with which the civil ruler is concerned.

The christological axis of the Reformer's thought is very evident
throughout this whole discussion. The position central to Zwingli's
theology as a whole becomes both the basis and the justification of
civil government. It is the foundation of law. On this ground one
can begin to understand the relations between church and state.
Zwingli, of course, was not the first Christian theologian to deal
with this problem. St. Augustine and St. Thomas, for example,
both treated the question at length. But even if one takes the
whole history of this discussion into account, it would seem that
Zwingli, through his dialectical approach, contributes something new. Divine justice invites us to consider man's life in the
fullness of what is human. Human justice obliges us to look toward the divine law from which the human gets its meaning. If
we do not grasp the dialectical movement in Zwingli's thought,
we do not understand it at all.

It is because this dialectic is not properly understood, or even
noticed, that some authors accuse the Reformer of confusing
church and state. Setting aside historical developments in which
extraneous factors played their part, we believe that this accu-
sation is not to the point. In his writings, Zwingli always distinguished clearly between the two. But just as church discipline
is administered on the basis of human justice, so the magistrate,
when he intervenes in ecclesiastical affairs, does so as a church
member. Although the two realms are distinct, they interpene-
trate each other dialectically.

This theory of the relations between church and state is
fundamentally what was worked out in practice in Calvin's
Geneva. Not without reason, Walther Koehler has suggested that
the Zurich domestic relations court (*Zürcher Ehegericht*) was the
real forerunner of the Genevan Consistory.[35]

Property and Usury

The end of the treatise *On Divine and Human Justice* deals with the problems of private property and the loan of money at interest. It is not irrelevant to deal with these matters as this study draws to a close.

For Zwingli, private property is a consequence of sin. It is the result of man's violation of the commandment to love his neighbor as he loves himself. Why so? Because if men loved each other, those who had an abundance of goods would help those who did not have enough. But this is not what happens. On the contrary, we egoistically hoard what God has generously given us. Private property thus came into being as a direct result of our sinful relation to others. We must not, of course, confuse Zwingli's position with that of a man like Proud'hon, who said that "property is robbery." Proud'hon's statement makes the existence of private property as such a presupposition, for how else could it be stolen? One only steals what already belongs to others, not what one is freely given.

Even if man were not sinful by nature, Zwingli holds that to convert God's gifts into private property would be a sin in itself.[36] Christ spoke truly when he spoke of the unrighteousness of riches (Luke 16:9). It is wrong for us to consider ourselves owners of God's gifts and to divert these gifts to our own private purposes. No one, Zwingli adds, is exempt from this sin, not even the beggar.

But since private property is a fact the magistrate must take account of it. The authorities cannot force people to give up their property even though divine justice demands it. How should the believer behave in such circumstances? He must be aware of the situation, and must realize that his "property" really belongs to God and is lent him by God to be used in God's service. The Christian will possess as if he did not possess (cf. 1 Cor. 7:30). "Apart from this," says Zwingli, "I cannot understand how a rich man can be a believer, because he will inevitably set his heart on earthly treasures instead of using them according to God's will."[37] It naturally follows that a true believer ought to lend money without collateral and without interest (Exod. 22:25; Luke 6:35).

But the fact that God commands us to lend without interest does not mean that a borrower who has agreed to pay interest can later refuse to do so. If a man borrows money at interest and subscribes to a legal contract, he must pay at the time the payment is due. Otherwise, he will disturb the peace and order of the community. This, of course, only concerns the realm of human justice which ought to have laws covering such matters. Interest under such laws should not exceed five per cent. If a man refuses to pay, he is actually guilty of sin against God, for in the human realm it is God's will that each man should have what is due him.

The function of the authorities in this area is to redress grievances. Those who want to lend their money should have a valuation made of their capital wealth and arrange each year to collect an amount of income that is within the requirements of the law. This way of dealing with the matter "will prevent many from sinning more, in the question of interest, than can be allowed to human weakness."[38] But, having said this, men must remember that divine justice is not to be ignored in business transactions. We must not forget that just as God feeds the birds he will provide for the needs of his children. When human justice is abused, indeed, it comes from a lack of faith and from ignorance of the requirements of divine justice. Therefore the magistrate must settle what interest rates are to be for the protection of borrowers and lenders alike. And if authorities consent to abusive rates, they can and should be impeached in court.

"Here," says Zwingli, "is my opinion about this unpleasant business of interest. . . Men must not let society descend into anarchy over poor handling of the question of material possessions. If the state of affairs troubles anybody with regard to God's commands, a solution must be found through regular and legal channels. For certainly Christ's teaching cannot be invoked for the purpose of causing social disorder."[39]

VI

IN CONCLUSION

We have now studied, all too briefly, some of the important features of Zwingli's theology. We have tried to look at this theology in a fresh way. We have sought to return to the primary sources and to be independent of traditional interpretations which have tended too much to make Zwingli everywhere simply "Zwinglian." It is our hope that the result has been to exhibit the Reformer of Zurich in a new light.

If this work has been on too small a scale for the thoroughness and detailed treatment that our subject deserves, it may still be hoped that it has been complete enough to introduce Zwingli to those who did not know him before, or to assist those who knew him imperfectly. Above all, what has been said has been enough, hopefully, to show that Zwingli was an authentic Reformed theologian in the broadest, as well as the most precise, sense of that term.

If a Reformed theologian is one who relies exclusively on the Word of God in Holy Scripture, who regards the visible church as the church of Christ in the fullest sense of the word and believes that Scripture gives guidance concerning its structure, who considers the ministries, including the ministry of discipline, as essential to the very being of the church, and who expounds a theory of government, politics, and social ethics in relation to the universal kingship of Christ, then Zwingli deserves that name. Indeed, he may have been the first to deserve it.[40]

Zwingli Literature

BIOGRAPHIES

Oskar Farner, *Zwingli the Reformer,* translated by D. G. Sear from *Huldrych Zwingli, der schweizerische Reformator.* New York: Philosophical Library, 1952 (German edition, Emmishofen: Johannes Blanke Verlag, 1917).

Samuel Macauley Jackson, *Huldreich Zwingli.* New York: G. P. Putnam's Sons, 1901.

Jaques Courvoisier, *Zwingli.* Genève: Labor et Fides, 1947.

Oskar Farner, *Huldrych Zwingli,* 4 vols. Zürich: Zwingli-Verlag, 1943-1960.

Walther Koehler, *Huldrych Zwingli.* Leipzig: Koehler & Amelang, 1943.

WORKS OF ZWINGLI

Huldreich Zwinglis Sämtliche Werke (Corpus reformatorum, vols. 88 ff.) (in course of publication). Leipzig: Heinsius, from 1905.

Huldreich Zwinglis Werke, Ausgabe durch Schuler und Schulthess, 8 vols. Zürich: Friedrich Schulthess, 1828.

Zwingli Hauptschriften, bearbeitet von Fritz Blanke, Oskar Farner, Rudolf Pfister (in course of publication). Zürich: Zwingli-Verlag, 1940.

Aus Zwinglis Predigten, bearbeitet von Oskar Farner. Zürich: Verlag Berichthaus, 1957.

TEXTS TRANSLATED INTO ENGLISH

Zwingli and Bullinger, Library of Christian Classics, vol. XXIV. Philadelphia: The Westminster Press, 1953.

The Latin Works of Huldreich Zwingli, together with selections from his German works, 2 vols. Vol. 1, ed. by Samuel Macauley Jackson (New York: G. P. Putnam's Sons, 1912); vol. 2, ed. by William John Hinkle (Philadelphia: The Heidelberg Press, 1922).

Notes and Acknowledgments

Introduction

1. Oskar Farner, *Huldrych Zwingli*, vol. I, p. 74. Zürich: Zwingli-Verlag, 1943.
2. *Ibid.*, p. 93.
3. *Huldreich Zwinglis Werke*, Schuler and Schulthess edition, vol. IV, pp. 92-93. Zürich: Friedrich Schulthess, 1828. Quotations from this edition are hereafter indicated S. E.g., S IV 98 means Schuler and Schulthess edition, vol. IV, p. 98.
4. Farner, *op. cit.*, p. 99.
5. Walther Koehler, *Huldrych Zwingli*, p. 13. Leipzig: Koehler & Amelang, 1943.
6. Farner, *op. cit.*, vol. II, p. 44.
7. *Huldreich Zwinglis Sämtliche Werke (Corpus reformatorum)*, vol. I, p. 169, line 23; pp. 171 ff. Leipzig: Heinsius, 1905. Unless otherwise indicated Zwingli quotations are from this edition and are simply listed by volume, page, and line. E.g., III 639/15-18 means this edition, vol. III, page 639, lines 15-18.
8. S IIb 298
9. Koehler, *op. cit.*, p. 66.
10. Farner, *op. cit.*, vol. II, p. 322.
11. *Ibid.*, pp. 324, 328; cf. Koehler, *op. cit.*, p. 64.
12. Arthur Rich, *Die Anfänge der Theologie Huldrych Zwinglis*. Zürich: Zwingli-Verlag, 1949.
13. Oswald Myconius, *Vita Huldrici Zwinglii. Vitae quatuor reformatorum*, p. 5. Berlin: Neander, 1841.
14. III 40/1-22, *passim*
15. *Heinrich Bullingers Reformationsgeschichte*, vol. I, pp. 289-291. Frauenfeld: J. J. Hottinger und H. H. Vögeli, 1898.
16. Walther Koehler, *Zürcher Ehegericht und Genfer Konsistorium*. Leipzig: Heinsius, 1932-1942.
17. Letter to Konrad Sam. XI 157/9-10
18. Walther Koehler, *Das Buch der Reformation Huldrych Zwinglis*, pp. 312 ff. München: Reinhardt, 1931.
   One may notice that, subsequently, Protestant politicians (for instance,

Calvin and Coligny) were always in favor of such resistance to a central European empire, that Gustavus Adolphus, later on, fought for the same cause, and that Great Britian's policy (as a Protestant country) has always been aimed at a balance of powers in Europe. On the other hand, Roman Catholic sovereigns have aimed at European domination: Charles the Fifth, Philip II, Louis XIV, Napoleon.

It is perhaps interesting to compare Zwingli's attitude, "Papacy and Empire are both from Rome," and what Karl Barth said, during World War II: "The character of the Swiss Confederation depends on its independence and on its neutrality . . . as a stabilizing element between powerful neighbors. War between the Axis and England is not at all a conflict between two imperialisms. One cannot reproach England for seeking to maintain the European equilibrium, for its own benefit. On the contrary, it is for the sake of this that England went to war against Germany. Nowadays, Switzerland, as a stable element between imperialisms, works for European equilibrium in being neutral. Switzerland ought to know that at this moment (1942) its neutrality is only threatened from one side. The other side, in its own way, fights and endures for the very cause which is that of the Swiss Confederation." Karl Barth, *Eine Schweizer Stimme*, p. 216. Zollikon-Zürich: Evangelischer Verlag AG., 1945.

19. Koehler, *Das Buch der Reformation Huldrych Zwinglis*, p. 346.
20. Ernst Gagliardi, *Histoire de la Suisse*, vol. I, p. 325. Lausanne: Payot, 1925.

I. The Word of God

1. III 639/15-18
2. Zwingli notices that St. Paul says the same thing in Acts 17:28. If the Apostle quotes a pagan poet, it is not because he credits him with authority equal to that of the biblical writers; rather it is to show "where one can find what the Spirit of God has sought to say through them." III 645/35; 646/2
3. I 344
4. III 643/1-3, 20-21, 24-27
5. III 654/28; 655/27-28
6. III 656
7. I 345/14-15
8. I 345
9. I 347/26-28
10. I 347/29-30
11. I 352/6-10
12. I 352/28-30
13. Here Zwingli uses the word *Brest*, which means "wound," "mutilation," or "illness."
14. I 338/23-25
15. I 365/24-25
16. I 366
17. I 374/23-26
18. II 79

19. II 76
20. II 79
21. II 27/17-20
22. III 681
23. II 37; III 691
24. III 695 f.
25. III 691
26. I 132/14-15; 133/8
27. Elsewhere Zwingli points out that when the fear of God makes us happy rather than sad this is a sign that the Word is acting in us and that the good news is reaching us. II 23
28. II 24/8-10; III 643
29. II 72
30. I 261/9-14; 262/29-31
31. I 319
32. III 642
33. II 25/17-18
34. III 488/6-8
35. I 353/8-13
36. S I 64; I 355/5-6
37. II 23
38. I 358
39. II 18/21-27
40. II 45
41. I 365/26-27
42. I 358/22-25
43. I 359
44. I 361/9-10
45. I 361/31-32
46. II 18/19-21
47. I 364
48. II 74
49. II 75/10-11
50. II 324/7-8
51. I 365/30-32
52. I 371/8-10
53. I 372/16-17
54. I 375/6-7
55. I 376/25
56. II 44/12-15
57. III 721
58. II 47; cf. II 643
59. II 22
60. I 381/1-4
61. I 379

II. The Christological Axis

1. II 14 ff.
2. II 30
3. II 32/13-14
4. II 34/27-28
5. II 43
6. II 43/22-23
7. II 45
8. I 167/14-22; 168
9. In allusion to the mercenary service of Swiss abroad and to the allowance paid by foreign princes to their recruiting agents in Switzerland. I 168/9-15; 169/5-9
10. Nicholas of Flue, after he had left his family to live as a hermit in the mountains, succeeded in maintaining peace among the Swiss cantons when they were on the point of slipping into civil war after a victorious campaign against the Duke of Burgundy.
11. III 103/22-27
12. III 657/23-24, 27-30
13. III 112/22-25
14. II 521/13
15. II 649/5-6
16. III 640/21-23
17. III 667/30; 668/10
18. III 668/23-25
19. III 675/29-30
20. III 667
21. III 681/30-31
22. Cf. Rudolf Pfister, *Die Seligkeit erwählter Heiden bei Zwingli*. Zollikon-Zürich: Evangelischer Verlag AG., 1952.
23. Cf. Gottfried W. Locher, *Die Theologie Huldrych Zwinglis im Lichte seiner Christologie*. Zürich: Zwingli-Verlag, 1952.
24. S IV 98
25. S IV 143
26. *Der evangelische Glaube nach den Hauptschriften der Reformatoren*, Vol. II, *Zwingli*, pp. 304-305. Tübingen: J. C. B. Mohr, 1919.
27. Locher, *op. cit.*, pp. 44-45.
28. V 618-619

III. The Church

1. S IV 3
2. *Ibid.*
3. Gottfried W. Locher, "Die Prädestinationslehre Huldrych Zwinglis," *Theologische Zeitschrift*, Jahrgang 12 (1956), pp. 526-548.
4. *Ibid.*, p. 537.
5. S IV 115

6. S IV 111
7. Locher, *op. cit.*, p. 538.
8. VI/1 175
9. S IV 123; cf. S IV 7
10. VI/1 177/7-10
11. VI/1 177/19-20
12. VI/1 177
13. *Institutes of the Christian Religion,* 4.1.8.
14. VI/1 180/18-20
15. Cf. Pfister, *Die Seligkeit erwählter Heiden bei Zwingli.*
16. Locher, *op. cit.*, p. 544.
17. VI/1 180
18. VI/1 155-164
19. VI/1 163/8-10, 23-25; 163/30; 164/4; 167/11-13; 168/32-35; 169/2-5; 170/6-8
20. VI/1 165 f. This quotation occurs in the midst of the passages cited above in note 19.
21. II 58/10-12
22. III 744
23. III 751/12-13
24. *Institutes,* 4.1.7-9.
25. *Ibid.,* 4.1.9.
26. II 56/17-18; 57/34; 58/1
27. III 744/15-18
28. III 745-747
29. III 750/23-24
30. III 751/19-21
31. Calvin will say the same thing; cf. *Institutes,* 4.1.13.
32. III 756-757
33. III 756
34. III 756/34-35
35. VI/1 489
36. S IV 8
37. S IV 58
38. J. L. Leuba, *L'institution et l'évènement.* Neuchâtel: Delachaux et Niestlé, 1950.
39. III 36/7-11
40. The meaning is the same as in Ephesians 3:15.
41. IV 384/20-21
42. IV 432
43. The ministerial commission can be given by the community as a whole acting as an electoral body (Acts 1:24), by the Apostles as such (Acts 8:7), or even by a single Apostle (Titus 1:5). IV 426
44. IV 427/2-5
45. IV 390
46. Calvin will say the same thing; cf. *Institutes,* 4.1.5.
47. IV 398/1-2
48. IV 430/1-3
49. IV 397/35

50. III 12/23-27
51. IV 416
52. III 13
53. II 522
54. Cf. Jaques Courvoisier, *La notion d'Église chez Bucer*, p. 88. Paris: Alcan, 1933.
55. Roger Ley, *Kirchenzucht bei Zwingli*, p. 109 (note). Zürich: Zwingli-Verlag, 1948.
56. II 276/25-28
57. Ley, *op. cit.*, p. 23, *passim*.
58. II 277/27-28
59. Ley, *op. cit.*, p. 46.
60. *Ibid.*, pp. 64 ff.; S VI 1 333-342; S VI 2 146-149
61. Cf. ch. V.
62. *Von der wahren Seelsorge*, 1538, LIIIb; cf. Courvoisier, *op. cit.*, p. 108.
63. Ley, *op. cit.*, p. 16.
64. *Ibid.*, p. 90.
65. *Ibid.*, p. 101.

IV. The Sacraments

1. III 757/10-20
2. III 761/20-22
3. III 761/22-29
4. III 761/32-38
5. III 763
6. III 768
7. III 765
8. III 764
9. VI/1 162 ff. (cf. above, p. 50)
10. IV 207; VI/1 31-32
11. IV 383/19-21
12. III 773/1-7
13. III 773
14. III 775/30
15. III 777/18-20
16. III 777/7-8
17. III 780/36-41
18. III 782/26-32
19. III 785/33-41
20. III 786
21. V 588
22. V 618/9-18
23. V 625/8-10
24. The so-called *extra calvinisticum* is to be found here. This played an important part in Calvin's thought; cf. *Institutes*, 2.13.4, and sermon on Eph. 1:15-16; *Calvini opera*, 51.3 and 18.
25. V 695/12; 698/2

26. *Institutes,* 4.17.12; "Traité de la Sainte Cène," *Calvini opera,* 5. 452.
27. S IV 51
28. S IV 11
29. III 789/9-13
30. In the treatise "Von dem widerchristlichen Missbrauch des Herrn Brot und Kelch."
31. Honius was a Dutch lawyer who, in a letter probably intended for Erasmus, concluded, after a comparative study of John 6:30 and 1 Corinthians 10:16, that there is no *manducatio oris* in the Lord's Supper, but only a *manducatio fidei.* Hinne Rode, rector of the Hieronimian School in Utrecht, carried this letter to Luther and later showed it to Zwingli. In this connection, Zwingli notes that in Scripture "is" quite often means "signifies," as in Genesis 41:26; Luke 8:11; John 15:1. Cf. III 793
32. III 793-799
33. 799-801
34. VI/1 481/28-29
35. S IV 56. In his discussion of Zwingli's doctrine of the Eucharist, Calvin does not mention this aspect of Zwingli's thought, a fact which, in our opinion, reduces the value of Calvin's judgment. Fritz Blanke is probably right in speculating that Calvin had not read the *Fidei Ratio;* cf. Fritz Blanke, *Calvins Urteile über Zwingli, Zwingliana,* Bd. XI, Heft 2, Nr. 2, p. 87. Zürich, 1959.
36. III 802/8-9
37. III 348/11-17
38. III 802
39. III 348/20-22
40. III 349/15-17
41. Julius Schweizer, *Reformierte Abendmahlsgestaltung in der Schau Zwinglis.* Basel: Verlag Friedrich Reinhardt AG., 1954.
42. *Ibid.,* pp. 84-85.
43. *Ibid.,* p. 91.
44. *Ibid.,* p. 103; IV 22/9-11
45. For example, Calvin seems to have been totally unaware of the ecclesial dimension of Zwingli's thought. Otherwise it is impossible to understand how Calvin could have written that the views of Zwingli and Oecolampadius on the Eucharist were "naked" and "empty" figures. It is true that Calvin admits that Luther's opinion of Zwingli turned him away from the Zürich Reformer to such an extent that he had not read anything from Zwingli's pen for some time (IX 51; cf. Blanke, *op. cit.,* p. 84). Calvin thus trusted Luther's opinion and considered him obviously superior to Zwingli (XI 24; cf. Blanke, *op. cit.,* p. 68). As a result, generation after generation of Lutherans and Calvinists have repeated the same mistake. So far as the ecclesial dimension of Zwingli's thought is concerned, it seems not to have been noticed, expounded, or developed by Reformed theologians. The only possible exception is Karl Barth, who nevertheless does not seem to feel any debt to Zwingli at this point. (IX 51 and XI 24 are from *Calvini opera.*)
46. III 349/1-2

V. Church and State

1. Cf. Heinrich Schmid, *Zwinglis Lehre von der göttlichen und menschlichen Gerechtigkeit* (Zürich: Zwingli-Verlag, 1959); Alfred Farner, *Die Lehre von Kirche und Staat bei Zwingli* (Tübingen: J. C. B. Mohr, 1930); and Ley, *Kirchenzucht bei Zwingli.*
2. Cf. chap. II.
3. II 479
4. II 481
5. II 79/11-12, 15-17
6. Cf. chap. I.
7. II 262/25-26
8. II 492/16; II 324
9. II 325/16; 325/29; 326/3; 326/9-10
10. II 492/14 (literally, "sugared")
11. II 482
12. II 485
13. II 486/21-23
14. II 486—487
15. II 488/2-4
16. II 489
17. II 485
18. II 501/19
19. II 344/30—345/3
20. II 344/27-28
21. II 345
22. II 346/9-10
23. II 301/15-16
24. II 310
25. II 308/8
26. II 321—322
27. II 497
28. II 304/8-9, 18-22
29. II 504/12-13
30. II 323/25-26; 324/4-8
31. II 334/22
32. II 337/15
33. II 329/3-5, 5-6; 330/10-14
34. II 330/22-23; 330/29—331/3; 330/10-11
35. Koehler, *Zürcher Ehegericht und Genfer Konsistorium.*
36. II 511
37. II 516/12-15
38. II 518/11-13
39. II 519/11; 520/15-20
40. Cf. Jaques Courvoisier, "Zwingli et Karl Barth," in *Antwort: Karl Barth zum siebzigsten Geburtstag,* pp. 369-387. Zollikon-Zürich: Evangelischer Verlag AG., 1956.